HEALTH REPORTS:
DISEASES AND DISORDERS

FOOD POISONING AND FOODBORNE DISEASES

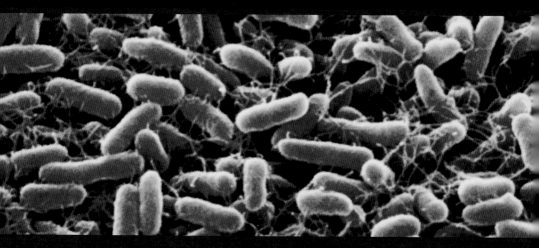

ELAINE LANDAU

TFCB TWENTY-FIRST CENTURY BOOKS
MINNEAPOLIS

Twenty-First Century Books
A division of Lerner Publishing Group, Inc.
241 First Avenue North
Minneapolis, MN 55401 U.S.A.

Website address: www.lernerbooks.com

Library of Congress Cataloging-in-Publication Data

Landau, Elaine.
        Food poisoning and foodborne diseases / by Elaine Landau.
             p.   cm. — (USA TODAY health reports: Diseases and disorders)
        Includes bibliographical references and index.
        ISBN 978–0–8225–7290–9 (lib. bdg. : alk. paper)
        1. Foodborne diseases—Juvenile literature. 2. Food poisoning—Juvenile
        literature. I. Title.
        RC143.L36 2011
        615.9'54—dc22   2009020325

Manufactured in the United States of America
1 – DP – 7/15/10

CONTENTS

USA TODAY
HEALTH REPORTS:
DISEASES AND DISORDERS

CHAPTER ONE

WHEN GOOD FOOD GOES BAD

I t was nearly Thanksgiving 2008, and just about everyone in South Burlington, Vermont, was getting ready to celebrate. The stores were well stocked with food, and people were busy planning their holiday menus. But one seven-year-old boy named Christopher was too sick to even think about food or the holidays.

Christopher had become ill on November 25 after eating some cheese and peanut butter sandwich crackers. He'd been hungry, and at the time, it seemed like a healthy enough snack. Less than a day later, he began to develop some very distressing symptoms. These included vomiting and painful stomach cramps. He also had diarrhea with blood in it.

The doctor who examined Christopher sent the boy directly to a hospital, where he remained for six days. The doctors there soon suspected that a foodborne illness was the problem, and they were right. Tests showed that young Christopher was suffering from the effects of Salmonella—a bacteria that is the most common form of foodborne illness in the United States.

USA TODAY Snapshots®

Taking goodies to school

More than half of children ages 8 to 13 bring a bag lunch three to five days a week. What they pack:

Snack cakes or cookies	73%
Fresh fruit or vegetables	73%
Meat or cheese sandwich	72%
Chips	71%
Peanut butter sandwich	59%

Source: Impulse Research for the American Dietetic Association/ConAgra Foods

By Julia Neyman and Marcy E. Mullins, USA TODAY, 2004

Christopher's illness came from the cheese and peanut butter crackers he'd eaten. His case was not an isolated incident, either. The child was just one of many victims of a broad-scale Salmonella *outbreak that had spread throughout much of the United States. The contamination had occurred at two or more peanut-processing plants owned by the same company. These facilities manufactured peanut butter and peanut paste, which were used in cookies, crackers, cakes, ice cream, and other peanut products sold throughout the country.*

The first reported illnesses had begun in September 2008. By the end of November, clusters of Salmonella *cases were reported in twelve states. On December 21, seventy-two-year-old Shirley Mae Almer died in a nursing home in Brainerd, Minnesota, after eating* Salmonella-*contaminated peanut butter later linked to the outbreak. By the beginning of February 2009, more than 575 cases and nine deaths in forty-three states had taken place.*

A DEADLY SNACK

Similar problems with food safety have occurred around the globe. One such incident took place on Bohol Island in the Philippines in 2005. There, a large number of first and second graders from San Jose Elementary School became extremely ill after eating fried cassava balls bought from local vendors. Cassava is a starchy root that grows in tropical regions. It can be prepared as a snack food and is also the source of tapioca.

The elementary schoolchildren in the Philippines ate the cassava as a snack during morning recess. Some of them said that the snack tasted bitter. They only had a few bites before they stopped eating it. Still, it was enough for them to feel ill before long.

www.usatoday.com

USA TODAY

News
SECTION A

February 3, 2009

From the Pages of USA TODAY

Health risks may reach far beyond reported victims

Like any mother facing a long day in the car and then on a plane with two young kids, ages 4 and 5, Jennifer Krieger of Alexandria, Va., was prepared. "I bought peanut butter crackers," she says, "thinking it would be a great healthy snack to take on the trip, easy to throw in my bag, and it won't go bad."

But things went bad, in ways that Krieger couldn't have imagined. A long-awaited Christmas vacation ski trip turned into a five-day vigil at a Colorado hospital after David Krieger, 4, got salmonellosis, a life-threatening infection caused by exposure to the *Salmonella* bacteria.

Federal officials say David, who has recovered, was one of more than 538 people across the nation who became sick after they ate contaminated peanut butter or foods containing tainted peanut paste made in a Peanut Corp. of America (PCA) manufacturing plant in Georgia. The infection also may have contributed to eight deaths, they say. Recalled products now number more than 1,700, including peanut butter crackers and many other snacks, although officials say major brands of peanut butter are not affected.

PCA is under a criminal investigation by the Food and Drug Administration [FDA]

and the Justice Department. A second congressional hearing on the recall is scheduled for Wednesday. The impact of the *Salmonella* contamination could reach well beyond the 538 people who got sick.

The conventional wisdom among epidemiologists, first outlined in a 2004 paper by Centers for Disease Control and Prevention [CDC] researcher Andrew Voetsch, is that for each case of salmonellosis that is reported, more than 38 other people get sick but don't go to their doctor or get tested. So this outbreak could be responsible for more than 20,000 illnesses.

Most fight off infection

Once ingested, the *Salmonella* bacteria start growing in the intestines. For the vast majority of people exposed, their bodies fight it off, and they never know they had it.

But depending on how many bacteria you have, or how old or sick you are, *Salmonella* can overwhelm the body's defenses and infect the colon, says Tim Dellit, an infectious-disease specialist at Harborview hospital in Seattle [Washington].

How hard *Salmonella* hits a given person depends on several factors: how much bacteria they consumed, how good their immune system is at fighting it off and how old or young they are.

But there's another interesting thing about *Salmonella*: There are thousands of different strains of the bacteria, and each seems to attack the body in a slightly different way, says Robert Tauxe of the CDC's division of foodborne, bacterial and mycotic [fungal] diseases.

There are *Salmonella* strains that hit younger people harder, and there are *Salmonellas* that hit older people harder. Some make boys sick more than girls; some, women more than men. In the ConAgra *Salmonella* outbreak associated with peanut butter in 2007, more than 25% of the cases showed up as a urinary tract infection in older women, researchers at the CDC found.

The current outbreak's potential impact on children likely has been reduced by the rise in peanut allergies in the USA. *Salmonella* is most dangerous for very young children.

Leslie Kurland of Hoosick, N.Y., went to culinary school, so she knows all about food safety and sanitation.

But it never occurred to her that peanut butter crackers could be the cause of the horrific bout of *Salmonella* that has son Gabriel, who is about to turn 2, on his second round of antibiotics.

Peanut butter and peanut paste, which are low in water and high in fat, are an almost perfect medium to preserve *Salmonella* bacteria even when they are exposed to heat.

That's a problem, because the "kill step" for peanut butter—the action that's supposed to ensure that it's free of harmful bacteria—is roasting, Donald Schaffner says.

That means that either the roasting of the contaminated products wasn't done at a high enough temperature or the peanut products were infected later in the process.

A recent FDA inspection found unsanitary conditions at the PCA plant. An FDA inspection report says PCA shipped products in 2007 and 2008 that tested positive for *Salmonella*.

In some situations, the products first tested positive and then negative—and then were shipped anyway. In others, the company shipped products before receiving positive test results, the FDA report says.

A wake-up call

Peanut paste goes through more heat exposure when it's baked in a cracker or some other kind of snack.

However, "*Salmonella* is a million times more heat-resistant when it's in peanut butter than when it's in chicken (a common carrier) or another high-moisture environment," Schaffner says.

"If there's anybody out there in the industry who's manufacturing nuts or nut butter of any kind, they really need to get on the stick and study the thermal processes they're using and document that it's effective against *Salmonella*."

For now, the only thing that's going to end this outbreak is for people to go through their cupboards and toss out potentially infected food.

"The shelf life of these products is months, if not years, in somebody's cupboard," says the CDC's Tauxe.

"They're going to be little time bombs going off for months unless people get rid of them."

—*Elizabeth Weise and Julie Schmit*

All the children who had the cassava balls began having stomach cramps. Vomiting and diarrhea soon followed. Because of the large number of young people affected, the children were immediately taken to four area hospitals. For some of the children, it was too late. Nearly thirty of them died as a result of what they ate. One of the vendors who sold the cassava balls to the school was a sixty-eight-year-old woman. She insisted that there was nothing wrong with the food. To prove her point, she ate some of the fried cassava balls herself. It wasn't long before she too was hospitalized in critical condition.

THE HAMBURGER NIGHTMARE

Perhaps one of the best-known and most widespread incidents of foodborne illness occurred in 1993 in the United States. A sizable

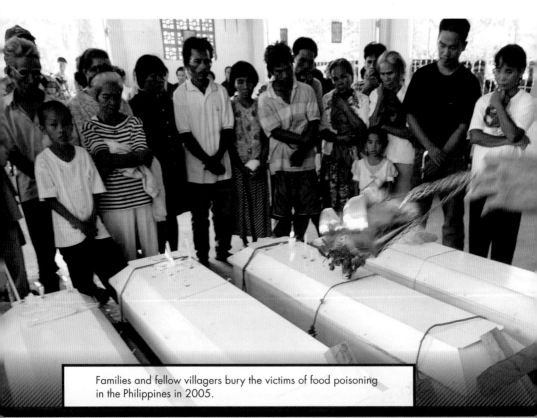

Families and fellow villagers bury the victims of food poisoning in the Philippines in 2005.

number of customers at a large hamburger chain became extremely ill after eating contaminated hamburgers. Those stricken included a large number of children. In one of the nation's worst foodborne illness outbreaks, about 600 people experienced symptoms and 144 became sufficiently ill to be hospitalized. Many of those affected were quite young, and four children died.

Among these was a two-year-old boy from Tacoma, Washington, who'd eaten a cheeseburger. He became nauseous later that evening. The next day, he had diarrhea, and from there, his condition worsened. Apparently, the hamburger he ate had been contaminated with *E. coli* O157:H7 bacteria. The little boy developed kidney failure and did not survive. Others who ate the contaminated meat developed chronic kidney failure and needed lifetime dialysis or a kidney transplant.

Among the survivors was ten-year-old Brianne Kiner. Much of the country had been rooting for her recovery. Like some of the others who'd eaten the tainted hamburgers, the girl had been taken to the hospital with flu-like symptoms and bloody diarrhea. She went into a coma in the hospital, and at that point, her doctors weren't sure that she'd survive. Finally, Brianne regained consciousness and began to improve. Though the girl's large intestine had to be removed and she'd have to deal with some future medical problems, her doctors predicted that she'd recover and go on to lead a normal life.

IT HAPPENS ALL TOO OFTEN

At times, the stories of foodborne illness and food poisoning may seem endless. In many cases, the person will experience nausea, vomiting, cramps, and diarrhea. These people will deal with a few days of discomfort, which may mean some time lost from school or from their jobs. For a fewer number of people, such as those who ate the contaminated hamburgers, the situation can be more serious.

www.usatoday.com

USA TODAY

Life
SECTION D

August 25, 1997

From the Pages of USA TODAY

For Colorado girl, misery lurked in a burger

Next week, almost two months to the day after Nicole Schlegelmilch cooked and ate a hamburger patty tainted with a lethal bacteria, the 12-year-old will start seventh grade. She knows how lucky she is.

She is one of 18 people in Colorado who ate hamburger contaminated with *E. coli* O157:H7, a bacteria that causes severe cramps, bloody diarrhea and, in the worst cases, can lead to kidney failure and death. The illnesses triggered the massive recall last week by Hudson Foods of 25 million pounds [11 million kilograms] of hamburger.

Nicole's mother, Ann, says it all started when she bought frozen burger patties on July 1 at a Safeway in Denver. The following day, she and a friend took Nicole and another girl on a camping trip to New Mexico. On the evening of July 3, Schlegelmilch says, the girls cooked dinner over a campfire. Nicole was in charge of grilling the burgers. She was the only one in the party who handled the meat raw and the only one who got sick. On July 8, she woke early with stomach cramps that progressed through the day to bloody diarrhea. The next day she was admitted to the hospital, where she stayed for three days.

Now, Nicole says she's feeling better, although she has lingering headaches. Her brush with a killer bug was scary. "I thought I was going to die," she says in a small voice. "I just felt really bad."

"Then we got lab results that confirmed *E. coli* O157:H7," a diagnosis that terrified her, [Schlegelmilch] says. "I knew it was deadly."

But in this case, it wasn't. Nicole, a sports lover, says she's looking forward to playing football this fall. She's a wide receiver, she says.

—*Anita Manning*

Nicole and Ann Schlegelmilch

In such cases, people may have to be hospitalized, and more serious medical complications as well as deaths may follow.

Food can become contaminated in numerous ways before it reaches our plates. According to the Centers for Disease Control and Prevention (CDC) of the U.S. Department of Health and Human Services, lots of different disease-causing microbes can contaminate foods, so there are many different foodborne diseases. At present, more than 250 have been identified. The majority are infections, caused by a variety of bacteria, viruses, and parasites. The rest are poisonings from harmful toxins or chemicals that contaminate food.

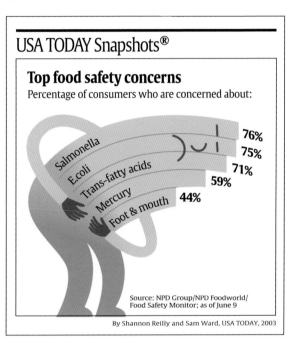

USA TODAY Snapshots®

Top food safety concerns

Percentage of consumers who are concerned about:

Salmonella — 76%
E.coli — 75%
Trans-fatty acids — 71%
Mercury — 59%
Foot & mouth — 44%

Source: NPD Group/NPD Foodworld/ Food Safety Monitor; as of June 9

By Shannon Reilly and Sam Ward, USA TODAY, 2003

TERRORIST FOOD THREATS

Outbreaks of foodborne disease can be frightening, unpleasant and, in some cases, even fatal. Most people would agree that an outbreak is bad enough when it happens accidentally, but what if a large number of people were deliberately made extremely ill through their food and water supplies? Ever since the September 11, 2001, terrorist attacks on the World Trade Center in New York and the Pentagon building in Washington, D.C., antiterrorism experts

have raised concerns about protecting the nation's food and water supply from terrorists. Government agents have alerted farmers throughout the United States to the possibility of an agroterrorist (a terrorist who attacks agriculture) threat. Such a threat would involve contaminating crops or livestock.

Antiterrorism experts have also suggested that the American water supply could be targeted. Water treatment plants in the United States disinfect and filter the tap water Americans drink. The fear is that a dangerous contaminant could be added to the water supply after the water has already been treated. As there are nearly two hundred thousand public and private water systems in the United States, it would be difficult to predict precisely where and when such an attack could take place.

Salad Bar Terrorists

In 1984 a radical cult in the United States, the Rajneeshees, caused more than 750 cases of *Salmonella* infection in a small Oregon town. *Salmonella* is a group of harmful bacteria that is sometimes transmitted through chicken and poultry. While the bacteria do not cause the bird to become ill while it is alive, it can make the people who eat the meat very sick. In this trial run, which was in preparation for a larger attack, the Rajneeshees contaminated several restaurant salad bars. The authorities did not even realize that the outbreak was intentional until the cult leader confessed the truth to the police more than a year later.

Attacks of this type could be devastating on a number of levels. Any city's health-care system would find it difficult to adequately handle several thousand extra cases of foodborne disease. It would be nearly impossible for a health-care system to find sufficient ventilators, beds, and skilled health-care workers to handle an emergency of that size. The fear of what might happen next could also cause widespread panic. The cost of emergency surveillance measures, medical treatment, and lost productivity would be staggering.

Hoping to avoid this scenario, the U.S. government since 9/11 has taken steps to enhance the systems protecting food and water. The Public Health Security and Bioterrorism Preparedness and Response Act of 2002 addresses general preparedness by pointing out where Americans need to strengthen defenses. It calls for the expansion of the Food Safety and Inspection Service and provides funding to research ways to quickly detect the contaminants in food and water. The good news is that in many cases, foodborne diseases are preventable. Much of the answer lies in practicing good food hygiene. While many people are concerned about food safety, not everyone is aware of the necessary steps to keep food free of contaminants and safe to eat. This is a book about how the food you eat can make you very sick. You'll learn how it can happen and what can be done to prevent it.

CHAPTER TWO

WAY BACK WHEN — THE HISTORY OF FOODBORNE DISEASE

P reventing widespread foodborne disease can be a complex and an often-tricky process. There are no quick or easy solutions. Epidemiologists, or public health officials who analyze and treat disease outbreaks, are always on the lookout for new problems and the best way to solve them. In addition, the fight against foodborne diseases changes over time. As researchers develop specific prevention strategies to fight and control one disease, new infectious agents emerge.

WHEN DID IT START?

Incidences of foodborne disease have occurred since early times. However, when people still lived in small isolated groups fairly far apart from one another, there were no large outbreaks. It was only as groups of people began to cluster together in cities, sharing communal water and handling food distributed to many people, that such problems surfaced.

In ancient times, people didn't understand why they became ill. They didn't know about bacteria, viruses, or the importance of sanitation. Often they simply assumed that they were being punished by the gods for some wrongdoing. People did not connect sanitation or cleanliness with good health.

Then Hippocrates, a physician who was born in about 460 B.C. in ancient Greece, began thinking along those lines. Hippocrates noted that clean water tasted better. He began boiling the water he used for his patients. He even took it one step further by designing a water filter of sorts. Hippocrates poured the water he boiled through a cloth bag to remove any remaining impurities. As a result of his advanced thinking and work, he later became known as the founder of medicine.

Though Hippocrates took some important steps in the right direction, he was only concerned with water that tasted or smelled bad. He did not realize that there were dangerous organisms lurking in the water that could not be seen with the naked eye.

The invention of the microscope in A.D. 1674 did not immediately improve the situation. It would take nearly another two hundred years for people to discover that some microscopic organisms could make them very sick. In the late 1850s, a French scientist named Louis Pasteur discovered that tiny organisms called germs were responsible for making many people ill.

Pasteur developed a process called pasteurization. In this process, liquids, such as milk and juice, are heated to kill germs. This was a tremendous advance in making food and beverages safe. Pasteurization saves millions of lives. In addition, Pasteur's work led to tremendous changes in hospital sanitation practices. As a result, it became much safer to be treated at hospitals.

TYPHOID FEVER

Typhoid fever is no longer a common foodborne disease in the United States. Yet this was not the case a century ago. Typhoid fever is caused by the *Salmonella typhi* bacteria. It is largely spread through food and water contaminated by the feces or urine of infected people. Typhoid fever was extremely common at the beginning of the twentieth century. It was considerably more dangerous then than it is today because antibiotics were not available then.

The typhoid fever bacteria invade the small intestine and from there enter the bloodstream. The white blood cells carry the bacteria to the liver, spleen, and bone marrow. When this happens,

the infected person will develop such symptoms as a high fever, headaches, and a loss of appetite. If left untreated, the person may later experience joint and muscle aches, chills, nosebleeds, mood swings, confusion, and hallucinations.

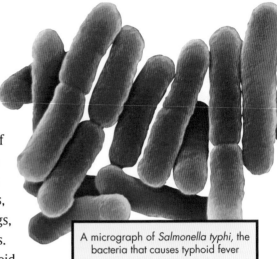

A micrograph of *Salmonella typhi*, the bacteria that causes typhoid fever

Scientists identified typhoid fever as a distinct disease in the early nineteenth century. By the 1880s, they had identified the organism, *Salmonella typhi*, that caused it. In 1900 most cases of typhoid fever resulted from contaminated drinking water. As water sanitation practices improved, the number of cases dropped. Nevertheless, the disease was still far from being eradicated. In 1900 more than twenty thousand people in the United States died of typhoid fever.

At the time, early epidemiologists studying typhoid fever also noticed an interesting fact about this illness. Cases of typhoid fever sometimes appeared in clusters, or groups of people, from the same area. This occurred even in places where the drinking water was not contaminated. This led epidemiologists to suspect that some individuals might be carriers of the disease. Epidemiologists later learned that between 2 and 5 percent of the people who've had the disease become chronic carriers. While these individuals no longer have any symptoms of the illness, they can still spread the germs. If any of these people work in food preparation, they can spread the disease to others.

Though the epidemiologists were on target, they didn't know this for certain. As of 1900, a typhoid fever carrier had never been identified. But that would change in 1906, after six people living in a home in Oyster Bay, New York, came down with typhoid fever. Anxious to find out how this could have occurred, the homeowner hired a sanitary engineer to investigate the cause. As a professional specializing in public health, the sanitary engineer was determined to get to the root of the cause.

After interviewing everyone in the house, the sanitary engineer decided to delve more deeply into the background of the family cook—a woman named Mary Mallon. He learned that typhoid fever had broken out at several other residences where she had been employed. She'd rarely held a position very long. The families she worked for would become ill, and Mary would quickly leave.

By then doctors were able to diagnose typhoid fever through laboratory tests. These tests were designed to detect the presence of *Salmonella typhi* from a stool or blood sample. When the sanitary engineer suggested that Mary submit a blood or stool sample to test for the disease, she became angry and ran away. She did not get very far. Mary Mallon was soon found by the police, who forcibly took her to a hospital so that a sample could be taken. The test results confirmed their suspicions. The first *Salmonella typhi* carrier had been identified. It was the cook, Mary Mallon. In the press, she soon became known as Typhoid Mary.

Mary did not like the idea of being labeled a carrier and refused to cooperate with the authorities. To protect others from being infected by her, she was detained in a quarantine facility on North Brother Island in New York's East River. After three years on the island, Mary promised to stop being a cook and begged to be released. If she kept her word, she would no longer be a danger to anyone.

Mary was released and shortly afterward seemed to disappear. However, Mary's job skills were limited. She had never been trained to be anything other than a cook and knew no other way to support herself. She began calling herself Mrs. Brown and went to work as a cook again. Mary was discovered when an outbreak of typhoid fever occurred at the Sloane Hospital for Women in New York City where she was employed in the kitchen. As it turned out, typhoid fever had also surfaced at several other places where Mary had worked before her job at Sloane.

Mary Mallon was arrested and taken back to North Brother Island, where she remained until she died twenty-three years later. Though officials did not like the idea of depriving Mary of her freedom, they felt it was their duty to protect the public's health.

Of course, modern outbreaks of typhoid fever are rare in industrialized countries such as the United States or Canada. The risk has been greatly reduced by advances in disinfecting drinking water, sewage treatment, and milk pasteurization. With the near eradication of typhoid fever in the United States, the disease is no longer viewed as a serious threat. While there is a vaccine to protect people against typhoid fever, it is usually only given to those traveling to countries where sanitation practices are less strict.

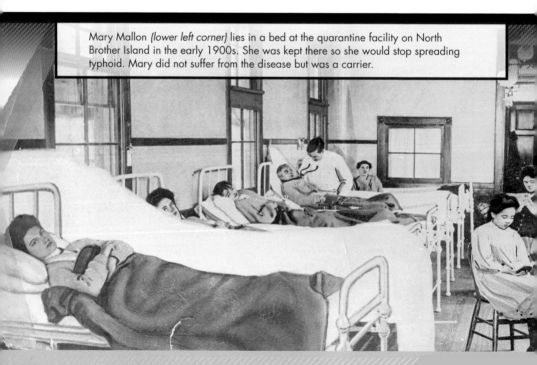

Mary Mallon *(lower left corner)* lies in a bed at the quarantine facility on North Brother Island in the early 1900s. She was kept there so she would stop spreading typhoid. Mary did not suffer from the disease but was a carrier.

Just When We Thought We Were Safe

Water and sewage are routinely treated to kill bacteria in the United States. So few Americans worry about coming down with typhoid fever. Yet during the winter of 1998 to 1999, epidemiologists in Miami-Dade County in southern Florida were presented with a troubling mystery. Suddenly, there was a rise in typhoid fever cases in the area. Something was up—for more than twenty years, the incidence of typhoid fever in the United States had been only one in one hundred thousand.

While the cases in Miami-Dade all occurred close to one another, those stricken seemed to have little in common. They did not know one another and received their water from at least four different water systems. They also had not engaged in any of the same social activities or eaten at the same restaurants.

So how did this happen? As it turned out, all those infected had drunk a frozen shake made with a tropical fruit called mamey. The mamey used was traced back to a frozen fruit concentrate made by two manufacturing plants in Guatemala and Honduras. Within a month of the first case of typhoid fever in Central America, the Florida Department of Agriculture and Consumer Services stopped the sale of frozen mamey in the state. Sure enough, no further cases were reported after that. This was the first report of a typhoid fever outbreak in the United States because of an imported food. Investigators stressed the importance of continued surveillance in identifying disease outbreaks and their causes.

Yet in many countries in Asia, Africa, and Latin America typhoid is still a problem. About 17 million people around the globe continue to be infected with the disease every year, and 600,000 of them die as a result of it. Nevertheless, typhoid fever can be effectively treated with antibiotics. In cases where antibiotics are administered early, the risk of death drops from between 10 and 15 percent to less than 1 percent.

CHOLERA

Cholera was another foodborne illness that caused a great deal of suffering throughout the world before the introduction of modern sanitation practices. Cholera spread largely by ship to many parts of the world in the early 1800s. Sailors would unknowingly load kegs of contaminated water onto vessels and carry the disease to distant ports.

Cholera strikes people with amazing speed. It appears as an intestinal infection caused by the bacteria *Vibrio cholerae*. The symptoms include watery diarrhea, vomiting, and leg cramps. A rapid loss of body fluids leads to dehydration and shock. In many early cases, its victims died within hours.

Much of Europe endured cholera epidemics in the early 1800s. By 1831 ships filled with immigrants brought the disease to North America. There was a cholera outbreak in Quebec, Canada, in the spring of 1832, and from there, it wasn't long before it spread to nearby Buffalo, New York. So many people there died of the disease that death carts soon patrolled the city's streets daily to pick up bodies. Those in charge of the carts would loudly cry out, "Bring out your dead," and soon the death carts overflowed with corpses from nearby homes.

Ships from Europe brought cholera to New York City as well. The situation became so bad there that the government declared June 29, 1832, as a day for prayer and fasting. Government officials felt so helpless in controlling the outbreak that there was little more they could think of to do.

In the mid-1800s, the United States was still a growing country. American pioneers headed west, and cholera went west as well. Many pioneers took the Oregon Trail west. The trail passed through the present-day states of Missouri, Kansas, Nebraska, Wyoming, Idaho, and Oregon. Pioneers faced many dangers along the trail, and one in ten died before reaching their destination. Those who died on the Oregon Trail were most likely to be killed by cholera. Some wagon trains lost as many as two-thirds of their members to the disease.

Because cholera was a quick killer, someone could get sick in the morning and be dead by nightfall. These wagon train pioneers were anxious to get to Oregon before winter, when travel became even more difficult. That left little time for mourning or funerals for cholera victims.

Often the wagon trains continued on, leaving a dying cholera victim by the side of the road with one other person attending him or her. The healthy individual, needing to catch up with the wagon train quickly, might begin digging the cholera victim's grave even before the person died. In some cases, the sick were simply left to die alongside the trail.

As the United States grew, new midwestern and western towns and cities sprang up across the land. These population centers were not immune to cholera either. Cholera appeared in Chicago, Illinois, in April 1849, after a large number of Irish immigrants arrived in the city. Nearly seven hundred people died of cholera that year. It was the highest death rate for a disease outbreak that the city had ever known.

www.usatoday.com

USA TODAY

Life

SECTION D

August 3, 2000

From the Pages of USA TODAY

The deciphered DNA [genetic code] of cholera could be the bug's downfall

Better vaccine might be ahead

Researchers have unraveled the genetic sequence for *Vibrio cholerae*, the bug that causes cholera, says a report out today.

Cholera is an extraordinarily rapid illness that causes diarrhea and, if left untreated, massive dehydration. It is caused by ingesting contaminated drinking water or food. Although rare in the USA, the disease still rages in other parts of the world, including Asia, Africa and Latin America.

With the building blocks of the bug's DNA in hand, scientists could design better tools to fight the disease and save thousands of lives each year, the researchers say.

Right now, doctors treat cholera by giving gallons of fluid to replace the water lost to diarrhea, he says. Without such treatment, about 60% of people with cholera would die.

The complete genome [map of the genes] of *V. cholerae* might lead to a better vaccine to prevent the disease, he says. The current vaccine often doesn't work.

A vaccine also might help prevent the explosive spread of cholera in refugee camps that form suddenly during times of conflict, researcher John Heidelberg says. Cholera hits fast and spreads like wildfire through such makeshift camps, which often don't have clean water or food.

The disease killed about 8,500 people last year, according to the World Health Organization.

Isolated cases of cholera occur in the USA, but the disease is unlikely to run wild because clean water is readily available, says Rita Colwell of the University of Maryland in Baltimore.

—Kathleen Fackelmann

Though cholera was a force to be reckoned with in the 1800s, it is exceedingly rare in the United States and other industrialized nations in the twenty-first century. Like typhoid fever, this deadly disease was largely conquered through improved sanitation. Modern sewage and water treatment systems virtually eliminated this deadly illness.

THE DISEASE DETECTIVES

In modern times, epidemiologists along with other researchers have done a great deal to stop outbreaks of present-day foodborne diseases. Epidemiologists act as disease detectives of sorts. They are faced with the puzzle of why people get sick and must put together the pieces to find the answers they need. Epidemiologists have to identify the source of the problem and try to make sure that the same thing doesn't happen again. One of the earliest examples of epidemiological research occurred in London, England, in the 1850s when a second cholera epidemic swept through the area.

At that time, a physician named John Snow did not believe the accepted thinking of the day that cholera was spread through the air. Instead, Snow felt certain that the disease was transmitted through contaminated water. Snow strongly suspected that the water pump at the corner of Broad Street and Cambridge Street in London was the source of the disease.

John Snow led research in Britain in the 1850s into the cause of cholera.

This was more than just a guess on Snow's part, as he'd done some valuable research to prove his point. Snow had reviewed the death records for area residents, and he had spoken to many of the surviving household members. He found that the vast majority of those who died of cholera lived near Broad Street and had obtained their drinking water from the pump.

One case did not fit the pattern, however. When Snow did some further investigation, he found that two women who lived about five miles [8 kilometers] from the Broad Street pump had also died of cholera. This struck Snow as very strange, since there was no cholera outbreak where they lived. Yet the mystery was solved after Snow visited the household of one of the women who died.

Snow learned that the woman who lived there had especially

Chlorine—Not Just for Swimming Pools

Untreated or contaminated water is often a source of foodborne disease. Water used by farmers to spray, wash, and maintain the attractive appearance of their fruits and vegetables must be free of harmful organisms. New practices in food safety were developed in the 1990s after outbreaks of *Salmonella* in 1991 were traced to cantaloupes that had been washed with contaminated water.

Melon growers developed the Melon Safety Plan. Under this plan, melons are washed with chlorinated water to kill any germs. The water used to make the ice for the melons to be shipped in is chlorinated as well. No records have been kept to report how extensively the plan was used, but there have been no further large outbreaks of *Salmonella* in cantaloupes since it was developed.

liked the taste of the water at the Broad Street pump and had arranged to have a large bottle of it brought to her daily. She had no idea that the delicious water she craved could lead to her death. The other woman in question turned out to be her niece. It seems that she had recently enjoyed some of the water from the Broad Street pump while visiting her aunt. She died shortly thereafter as well.

Snow shared his thinking with community leaders, and they agreed to remove the pump's handle. The handle was taken off on September 8, 1854, and sure enough, no further cholera deaths occurred in the area. In modern times, Snow has sometimes been referred to as the father of epidemiology.

EPIDEMIOLOGISTS AT WORK

Modern epidemiologists have followed John Snow's lead and continue to investigate outbreaks of foodborne disease. They work to stop such outbreaks and to prevent similar ones from occurring in the future. Epidemiologists learn of outbreaks of foodborne diseases in different ways. Sometimes information comes from a call to a local health department reporting that a number of people who ate at a particular event, such as a wedding reception or a church supper, have become ill. Other times a doctor will call the Centers for Disease Control and Prevention to report that an unusually large number of people have become ill with very similar symptoms. It can also happen when a particular health department receives an unusually large volume of calls regarding a possible outbreak.

The epidemiologist's job becomes harder when the people who've become sick are spread over a broad geographic area. The epidemiologist knows that these incidents may be connected even though there may only be a few cases in each state. Such outbreaks have become increasingly common in recent years because so much of the food Americans eat is nationally distributed. That makes it possible for contaminated food from one source to make people ill throughout the country. One such outbreak of foodborne illness involved a brand of nationally distributed ice cream. The contaminated ice cream made more than 250,000 people sick in a number of states. In these cases, epidemiologists have to employ new DNA fingerprinting techniques. They compare the DNA, the genetic material, of various strains of the disease-producing organisms to see if all the illnesses stem from the same source.

Part of the epidemiologist's investigation involves charting how many people have come down with the same symptoms, as well as when and where these people got sick. If the infectious agent that caused the problem is unknown, epidemiologists take blood or stool samples from the ill individuals and send them to a public health laboratory for a diagnosis. They conduct interviews to learn more about what the ill people ate in the days before their symptoms appeared.

The epidemiologist will look for common factors. For example, let's say that the eggnog served at a holiday party is suspected of being contaminated and of making those who drank it sick. The epidemiologist might interview forty people who were at the party— perhaps thirty of these became ill, while ten remained well. Everyone would be asked if they had eggnog along with the other foods served there. If the epidemiologist finds that the thirty people who drank the eggnog became ill while the ten who did not remained well, the epidemiologist then can conclude that the eggnog is probably the source of the problem. This conclusion will be strengthened if the epidemiologist can determine that those who had second and third helpings of eggnog were even more likely to become ill.

Once a contaminated food or beverage item has been identified in this manner, the epidemiologist will look more closely at its ingredients. Was the eggnog made with raw eggs? If this is the case, the eggs will be traced to the farm they came from by identifying where the eggs were purchased and who supplied them to that store or outlet. It's likely that other chickens at that farm are carrying the same strain of bacteria. If this is so, eggs from that farm can be pasteurized to prevent further outbreaks.

It is important to stop outbreaks of foodborne disease, and it can be done in different ways. Sometimes the producer will recall contaminated foods. When this happens, the contaminated product is taken off store shelves and people who purchased the product can return it for a refund. In 2009 a number of nationwide retail chain stores called millions of customers who bought peanut products. These consumers were warned that their purchases might be tainted with *Salmonella* bacteria. They were advised to immediately return or destroy the suspected foods. Sarah Klein, an attorney for the Center for Science in the Public Interest, a Washington, D.C., consumer advocacy group, praised these stores and urged other sellers to do the same. "Only retailers know who purchased a product," she noted in underscoring the steps needed to keep the public safe.

An epidemiologist talks to a family to try to discover what specific food caused a *Salmonella* outbreak in 2008.

USA TODAY

www.usatoday.com

USA TODAY

Money
SECTION B

January 24, 2009

From the Pages of USA TODAY

Peanut butter recall grows
Expanded to 2 years' worth of products

The recall of peanut butter and paste products made at a Georgia plant was expanded Wednesday to include two years of production, making it one of the largest recalls ever, the Food and Drug Administration says.

The expansion will engulf many more products beyond the 432, including crackers and cookies, already on a list kept by the FDA at www.fda.gov.

The FDA also Wednesday released a scathing report on conditions at the Peanut Corp. of America [PCA] plant linked to the *Salmonella* outbreak, and Rep. Rosa DeLauro, D-Conn., called on the Department of Justice to see if a criminal probe is warranted.

The tainted peanut products have been linked to 501 illnesses nationwide and may have led to eight deaths.

The FDA's report, covering a 14-day inspection, revealed poor sanitation, conditions that would allow *Salmonella* to spread, a gap in the roof through which

Other measures are employed to protect consumers as well. A restaurant or food-processing plant that is not following proper sanitation procedures will either have to improve its performance or the authorities will close it down. In still other cases, an infected food handler, such as the famous Typhoid Mary, will be forced to stop working with food.

The Centers for Disease Control and Prevention also plays an important role in keeping the nation's food supply safe. As part of the U.S. Public Health Service, the agency works closely with state health departments to identify and prevent outbreaks of foodborne disease. At times, the CDC will send a team into the field to conduct

Salmonella-contaminated water or bird feces could fall, the presence of roaches and failure by the firm to check that its peanut-roasting process killed *Salmonella*.

Previous checks of the plant by Georgia inspectors noted smaller sanitation infractions.

The most serious issue found by the FDA and reported Tuesday was that the plant in 2007 and 2008 sold peanut butter or other products that tested positive for *Salmonella* after retests came up negative. Such product should not have been sold, the FDA says.

Dozens of companies have recalled products, including Kellogg. Its auditor checked the plant last year, giving it a superior rating, spokeswoman Kris Charles says. The plant replaced its roof since last fall, so a half-inch [1-centimeter] gap found by the FDA may not have been there, the FDA's Stephen Sundlof says.

PCA's peanut butter was sold to institutions. Major-brand peanut butter sold in stores is not affected, the FDA says. PCA's peanut paste or butter went into hundreds of products such as crackers, cookies and ice cream.

Georgia lawmakers are considering requiring foodmakers to inform state officials about internal product-test results, says Tommy Irvin, commissioner of the Georgia Department of Agriculture.

PCA says it uses "reputable" labs for its product testing and doesn't agree with all of the FDA's observations on its inspection report.

"We have been devastated by this, and we have been working around the clock with the FDA to ensure any potentially unsafe products are removed from the market," said Stewart Parnell, PCA president. The Blakely, Ga., plant has closed.

—*Julie Schmit, Elizabeth Weise*

emergency field investigations of large or unusual outbreaks. CDC researchers also develop new methods to better identify the microbes that cause disease. The CDC shares the results of its investigations and research nationwide to coordinate efforts to enhance public health and safety.

Understanding what's behind foodborne disease outbreaks can sometimes lead to important changes in food storage and handling procedures. When disease outbreaks are properly publicized, consumers will learn more about food safety procedures. These measures can go a long way in keeping our food safe and enjoyable while reducing the risk of similar outbreaks.

www.usatoday.com

Money
SECTION B

June 18, 2008

From the Pages of USA TODAY

How modern science and old-fashioned detective work cracked the *Salmonella* case

The contamination of tomatoes with a rare strain of *Salmonella* has led to the largest outbreak of foodborne illnesses since *E. coli* in spinach killed five and sickened hundreds almost two years ago.

At least 277 people of all ages in 28 states and the District of Columbia have been sickened; 43 have been hospitalized. A nationwide recall of round, plum and Roma tomatoes has dealt a sharp blow to the $2.7 billion fresh-tomato market, costing the food industry tens of millions of dollars.

But it could have been a lot worse if a red flag hadn't been raised early in the outbreak last month by a public health nurse with good instincts in one of the nation's poorest, most remote regions.

Indeed, health officials say that because the first cluster of patients surfaced on the Navajo Nation in New Mexico, where they are served by a small, close-knit medical community, federal investigators were able to quickly identify the contaminated foods and take steps to contain the outbreak the past two weeks.

After being the first to recognize the signs of an emerging outbreak, the federal Indian Health Service staff played a key role in the search for the tainted food. "It was 21st-century molecular epidemiology and old-fashioned boot leather," says John Redd, the infectious disease branch chief with the Indian Health Service in Albuquerque. "You've got to get out from behind your desk and hit the road sometimes."

Over the next two days, cases appeared in several New Mexican counties. Some patients were Navajo, some were not. All were very ill. "That really starts ringing the bells," Paul Ettestad says. He contacted Ian Williams, chief of the outbreak team at the Centers for Disease Control and Prevention.

Cases were starting to pop up in Texas, too. "We had two cases reported out of Houston on the 22nd, and an additional 12 on the 23rd. Things moved pretty quickly," says Linda Gaul, head of the food-borne illness team at the Texas Department of State Health Services.

Then New Mexico posted the genetic fingerprints of its cases onto PulseNet, the CDC's computer disease-tracking network. Within hours, matches began to show up. The outbreak wasn't just in New Mexico and Texas, it was all over the country.

The common thread

Even though it was Memorial Day weekend, everyone mobilized to work. New Mexico, Texas, the CDC and the Indian Health Service began holding daily conference calls. As other states got patients, they joined in.

In a case like this, epidemiologists, the doctors who study outbreaks, pull out what they call a "shotgun survey." It's a long—in this case 22 pages—survey that covers just about anything a person might eat, drink or be exposed to that could cause such an illness.

"Shotgun, because it's like shooting in the dark to see what's there," says Texas' Gaul.

Enter the Indian Health Service again, charged with the task of administering the survey in the Navajo Nation, which by sheer chance seemed to have gotten the most cases in New Mexico.

"Our Indian Health nurses would drive two or three hours to try to find these people and when they couldn't find them, they'd have to go back," he says.

Also, each nurse had to painstakingly reconstruct everything the patient had eaten in the previous two weeks. "Nurses pulled out calendars for clients and said, 'Where were you? Who were you with? What meal did you have with that event? What did you do before the event, and what did you eat later in the day?'" says Houk.

To do that, a nurse was sent into a patient's home "and she literally pointed at every shelf on the refrigerator and every cabinet and asked, 'Did you eat anything on this shelf?' It's a difficult thing to do. It makes people feel anxious," Houk says.

But it did the trick. Even people who swear they didn't eat raw tomatoes remember they might have when asked about salsa or guacamole or a slice of tomato on a hamburger. On Saturday, with surveys coming in not only from New Mexico but a few other states as well, the percentage of patients who'd eaten fresh tomatoes stood at 75%, compared with an average of 68% random Americans. By Sunday, with more cases analyzed, the share shot up to 83%, Ettestad says.

Three days later FDA issued a warning for Texas and New Mexico. Five days later, with cases appearing across the nation, FDA made the warning national.

The agency was able to quickly announce where the tomatoes didn't come from because most tomato-growing areas weren't harvesting in late April when the first cases showed up. It soon became clear that mid-Florida and Mexico were the only major growing areas selling tomatoes at that point.

"In the past most food was produced and consumed locally, you wouldn't have much trouble figuring out where (tainted) food came from," he says.

Today, he says, having fresh, ripe, cheap tomatoes available in salads nationwide in April—inconceivable two generations ago—also means "the distribution is so broad that something (contaminated) can show up in 13 states the next day."

—Elizabeth Weise, with Julie Schmit

CHAPTER THREE

BUGS TO BEWARE OF

Four-year-old Jenny ate a contaminated hamburger. At first, the child complained of stomach cramps. Her mother thought it was probably just gas. But the next day, Jenny's stomach still hurt. She was never a child who complained, but she even felt too ill to go outside to play with her sisters. There were other symptoms too. She soon had diarrhea, which was reddish in color. She began vomiting as well.

The next day, Jenny's mother took her to their pediatrician, who felt fairly certain that Jenny had the flu. Her mother asked if the reddish color in her diarrhea could be blood. The pediatrician answered that it was not uncommon to see blood in the stools of a child who had the flu. Just in case, the doctor took a stool sample, but the results would take a few days.

It was the flu season, so Jenny's mother simply assumed that the doctor was correct. Yet Jenny's symptoms continued to worsen. She still had cramps, and she became extremely weak. She began to run a fever and became frighteningly pale. She also found it hard to urinate. The situation seemed serious, so Jenny's parents decided not to wait to see their pediatrician again. Instead, they drove Jenny to the emergency room of the local hospital.

By then the diarrhea and vomiting had taken its toll, and Jenny had become severely dehydrated. She was admitted to the hospital, where more blood tests were taken. The staff asked her parents questions about the food Jenny had eaten. They wanted to know what Jenny ate, when and where she ate it, and how much of it she had.

Jenny's blood test results weren't normal, and the doctors feared that her kidneys were affected. They suspected that Jenny had been infected with E. coli O157:H7 and that she had developed kidney problems. The tests confirmed that they were right. Jenny's parents were worried. In extreme cases, where the kidneys fail completely, children sometimes go into a coma or even die.

At first, the doctors weren't sure how well Jenny would do. She remained in the hospital, where she was carefully monitored and received several blood transfusions. When her kidneys failed to respond, she was temporarily put on a dialysis machine, which cleans the blood the way human kidneys do.

Before too long, Jenny improved enough to be released from the hospital. She was anemic (had a low number of red blood cells), and there were still some blood cells in her urine. She has recovered, although she'll need to be monitored for years for possible complications or kidney failure.

Just as foodborne diseases such as cholera and typhoid fever are largely conquered in industrialized nations, new infectious agents appear, and the fight for food safety continues. The foodborne diseases discussed in this chapter are infections that develop when people ingest bacteria and viruses, living infectious agents. Viruses are very tiny disease-producing organisms. They are the smallest life-form known and can be one hundred times smaller than bacteria. There are other differences between viruses and bacteria as well. Most bacteria can grow on a nonliving surface, but viruses need a living host in order to reproduce or multiply. Some bacteria and viruses can make people very sick. A number of the more troublesome causes of foodborne illness that have recently come to the public's attention are described here.

E. COLI O157:H7

E. coli O157:H7 is an infectious agent that people have come to dread since it was recognized as a cause of foodborne illness in 1982. Under

a microscope, *E. coli* O157:H7 appears to be just one of hundreds of strains of the bacteria *Escherichia coli*. The combination of numbers and letters in its name refer to the particular characteristics that distinguish it from other types of *E. coli*. Most *E. coli* strains are not harmful, but *E. coli* O157:H7 can be. It produces a dangerous toxin that can make people quite ill. *E. coli* O157:H7 most recently came to the public's attention when a number of outbreaks were traced to contaminated hamburgers. According to the Centers for Disease Control and Prevention, about seventy-three thousand cases of sickness caused by *E. coli* O157:H7 appear in the United States each year. They result in an estimated sixty-one deaths annually.

E. coli O157:H7 can live in the intestines of cattle that show no signs of illness. The contamination happens when the animal is slaughtered. If the animal is not slaughtered carefully and the meat is not carefully ground, these organisms in the intestine of the animal can become mixed into the beef that later becomes hamburger patties or meat loaf. The contaminated meat will not have an unusual look or bad smell.

E. coli O157:H7 can also get into raw milk. This can happen while the cow is being milked if the bacteria from cow manure are either on the cow's udder or on the equipment used to milk it.

Other ways *E. coli* O157:H7 has been known to be transmitted is through sprouts, lettuce, and unpasteurized juice. This happens when seeds or irrigation water or floodwater has been contaminated with cow manure. People have also contracted *E. coli* O157:H7 by swimming in or drinking contaminated water.

Besides these routes of transmission, the bacteria can also be passed from one person to another through the stools of an infected person. This is most likely to happen when parents or child care workers change the diapers of an infected toddler and fail to wash their hands afterward. It is not uncommon for young

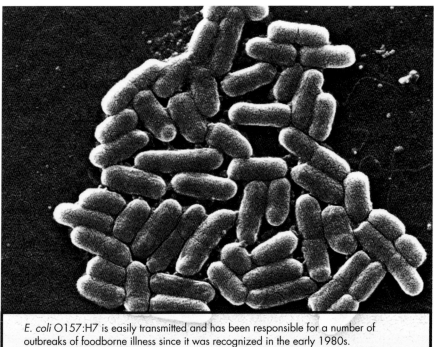

E. coli O157:H7 is easily transmitted and has been responsible for a number of outbreaks of foodborne illness since it was recognized in the early 1980s.

children to shed the bacteria in their feces up to two weeks after their symptoms are gone.

SYMPTOMS

Though sometimes there are no symptoms, someone infected with *E. coli* O157:H7 usually will experience bloody diarrhea and severe stomach cramps. Often the person will experience vomiting as well. In most cases, there is no fever and the illness is over in five to ten days. Infection with *E. coli* O157:H7 can be especially hard on both the elderly and very young children. One serious complication is hemolytic uremic syndrome (HUS). In this condition, the bacteria destroy red blood cells, which leads to kidney failure. HUS is the major cause of acute kidney failure in children in the United States. About 2 to 7 percent of *E. coli* O157:H7 infections lead to HUS.

www.usatoday.com

USA TODAY

News

SECTION A

April 13, 2007

From the Pages of USA TODAY

CDC reports *E. coli* cases are on the rise in leafy greens

Raw natural diet fuels new pattern of food illnesses

The deadly strain of *E. coli* responsible for hundreds of illnesses and at least three deaths last year was a leading culprit in the government's annual report on foodborne illnesses.

The preliminary report card shows that progress against some foodborne diseases has stalled, while cases of others considered under control are increasing.

The Morbidity and Mortality Report from the Centers for Disease Control and Prevention was released today. Based on data from 10 participating states, it gives a snapshot, but not a full picture, of the nation's foodborne illnesses, according to CDC director Julie Gerberding.

The biggest development was the blooming of *E. coli* O157:H7 in vegetables, she said. For decades meat, especially

ground beef, was the major source of *E. coli* illnesses. From 1996–98, there were 2.3 cases of this strain per 100,000 people. That number dropped to 0.9 by 2004, but was back up to 1.31 in 2006.

"Two years ago we were looking at what looked like a pretty good success story for *E. coli* O157:H7," said Robert Tauxe, deputy director of CDC's Foodborne, Bacterial and Mycotic Diseases division.

E. coli O157:H7 cases tied to ground beef are decreasing, thanks to major food-safety reforms by the meat industry, Tauxe said.

A massive 1993 *E. coli* outbreak tied to hamburgers sold at Jack-in-the-Box restaurants raised national awareness of the bacteria when four people died and more than 500 became ill.

DIAGNOSIS AND TREATMENT

E. coli O157:H7 is diagnosed by detecting the bacteria in an infected person's stool. The Centers for Disease Control and Prevention recommends that people with blood in their stools be tested for *E. coli* O157:H7.

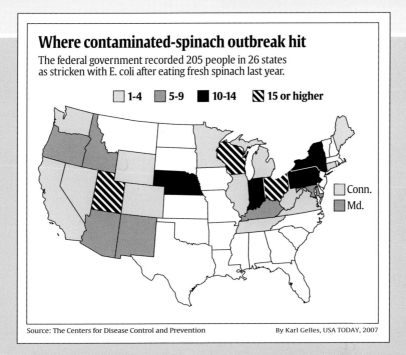

Where contaminated-spinach outbreak hit

The federal government recorded 205 people in 26 states as stricken with E. coli after eating fresh spinach last year.

☐ 1-4   ▨ 5-9   ■ 10-14   ▨ 15 or higher

☐ Conn.
▨ Md.

Source: The Centers for Disease Control and Prevention   By Karl Gelles, USA TODAY, 2007

In 2006, the presence of *E. coli* O157:H7 in ground beef was 0.17%, the same as in 2004 and 2005, according to U.S. Department of Agriculture's Food Safety Inspection Service data. But three major national outbreaks of the deadly O157:H7 strain in spinach and lettuce last year brought *E. coli* roaring back.

Fresh Express, the nation's largest producer of ready-to-eat greens, announced Thursday that it's awarding $2 million in research grants to the study of *E. coli* O157:H7 in lettuce and leafy greens.

"The desire for a raw natural diet is leading to a new pattern of foodborne illness," said Douglas Powell, a professor of food safety at Kansas State University in Manhattan [Kansas].

Oversight agencies need more money, said Caroline Smith DeWaal, food-safety director at the Center for Science in the Public Interest. "The FDA needs to have its budget dramatically increased," she said, adding the agency "is literally starving for resources."

—Elizabeth Weise

Most people will recover from infection with *E. coli* O157:H7 without any treatment. At one time, antibiotics were prescribed to treat it, but doctors began to suspect that some of these medications could contribute to kidney complications. In cases in which HUS develops, the situation can become life threatening. Ill individuals are usually treated in a hospital's intensive care unit. While a person is hospitalized with HUS, blood transfusions and kidney dialysis are frequently necessary.

In mild cases of infection with *E. coli* O157:H7, the ill person may have only experienced diarrhea and perhaps some vomiting. These people often recover completely. In cases where HUS has developed, the situation is considerably more serious. The patient may have abnormal kidney function even years later and may require ongoing dialysis. A small percentage of the patients that survive HUS will have other lifelong complications. These include high blood pressure, seizures, blindness, and paralysis.

SALMONELLA

Salmonella are rod-shaped, microscopic bacteria that cause an infection known as salmonellosis. About forty thousand cases of salmonellosis are reported in the United States each year. The actual number may even be twenty or thirty times higher since mild cases often go unreported. About six hundred people die every year as a result of salmonellosis. The illness tends to hit young children, the elderly, and those with compromised immune systems hardest.

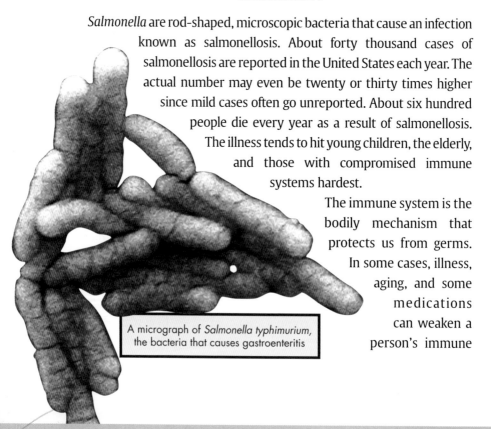

A micrograph of *Salmonella typhimurium*, the bacteria that causes gastroenteritis

The immune system is the bodily mechanism that protects us from germs. In some cases, illness, aging, and some medications can weaken a person's immune system. The immune systems of very young children have not had time to mature and are not as strong as those of older individuals.

Salmonella is transmitted to humans when they eat foods that have been contaminated by animal feces. As with *E. coli* O157:H7 bacteria, the contaminated food usually looks and smells fine. Therefore, there is no way of knowing that the food is bad. The foods most commonly contaminated by *Salmonella* are beef, poultry, eggs, and milk. Any food can become contaminated, however. An infected food handler can contaminate food if that person prepares food after using the restroom and neglects to wash his or her hands. *Salmonella* also can be transmitted through pets that have the bacteria in their feces. People can become infected if they do not wash their hands after cleaning up after their pet and then go on to prepare food that they eat.

SYMPTOMS

Among the most common symptoms of *Salmonella* are diarrhea, fever, headaches, and stomach cramps. In most cases, the symptoms begin to appear from twelve to seventy-two hours after infection. Most people remain sick with salmonellosis for four to seven days. Some cases of salmonellosis are more serious. At times, the diarrhea becomes so severe that the person becomes dehydrated and needs to be hospitalized.

Sometimes the infection can also spread from the intestines to the bloodstream. Blood can carry the infection as it circulates through the body. When this happens, the infected person may die if not treated immediately.

One widespread outbreak came to light in June of 1999 when a department of health in Oregon received some reports of salmonellosis. An investigation by the Oregon Public Health Division revealed that four ill people were part of a group of thirteen who had eaten at a brunch buffet in Portland. They had experienced diarrhea, vomiting, and fever. The four who became ill were the only ones who had the orange juice served at the buffet that day.

At about the same time, other people developed the same symptoms in both Washington State and Canada. Testing revealed that all those stricken were also suffering from *Salmonella* infection. After investigating, the Food and Drug Administration determined that the outbreaks were related. They were all linked to unpasteurized orange juice that had been distributed by a single company. The juice had been labeled "fresh squeezed orange juice" and had been distributed to numerous groceries and restaurants under different labels. At the end of June, the company voluntarily recalled its unpasteurized orange juice. By the time the outbreak was over, more than two hundred people had become ill.

DIAGNOSIS AND TREATMENT

The symptoms of a *Salmonella* infection are similar to many other kinds of illnesses. Laboratory tests have been designed to identify these bacteria. A sample of the ill person's stool is sent to a lab to be analyzed. Once it is determined that it is *Salmonella*, additional tests will reveal which strain it is. This is important for the doctor to know how best to treat it.

Many people with *Salmonella* infections recover without any treatment. However, if this infection is severe, a doctor will usually prescribe antibiotics. If an infected person becomes dehydrated as a result of severe diarrhea, that person may be given intravenous fluids.

While most people soon recover from salmonellosis, a small number will have long-term consequences from their bout with these bacteria. They develop Reiter's syndrome, which is characterized by joint pain, irritated eyes, and painful urination. This condition can also lead to chronic arthritis.

Look Out for Listeriosis

In recent years, the foodborne disease listeriosis has emerged as an important public health concern throughout the United States. Every year approximately twenty-five hundred people in the United States become seriously ill with listeriosis. Listeriosis is a serious infection that results from the bacteria *Listeria monocytogenes (right)*. This bacteria may be found in a wide range of raw foods, such as uncooked meats and vegetables. It is also frequently found in processed foods, such as meat cold cuts sold at deli counters. Soft cheeses and products made with unpasteurized milk may be another source of *Listeria*.

Listeriosis is largely characterized by fever and muscle aches. Often those infected feel as though they have a mild case of the flu. If the infection spreads to the central nervous system, the situation can become more serious. The ill person may experience headaches, confusion, balance problems, and convulsions.

The disease is especially dangerous for pregnant women. While some only become mildly ill, others experience serious complications. The illness can lead to miscarriage, stillbirth, premature delivery, or infection in the newborn. For some reason, pregnant women are about twenty times more likely than other healthy women to get listeriosis. Nearly one-third of all listeriosis cases occur during pregnancy.

www.usatoday.com

Money
SECTION B

December 5, 2006

From the Pages of USA TODAY

Restaurants say cooking makes their chicken safe

But improper handling can spread the bacteria

Uncooked chicken purchased at supermarkets may suddenly be suspect—but just how safe is the cooked chicken you buy at a restaurant?

There will be plenty of consumers asking that question today following release of a *Consumer Reports* study that shows 83% of the fresh, broiler chickens it bought at supermarkets of all types last spring were tainted with *Salmonella* or *Campylobacter* bacteria.

The *Consumer Reports* study did not test chicken at restaurants, but interviews with nutritionists, restaurant consultants and other food experts indicate restaurant-made chicken generally is safe.

And that safety factor typically—but not always—increases at larger chains and may decrease at mom-and-pop restaurants that may be less careful about food preparation.

"These bacteria are susceptible to heat. At 160 degrees [F, or 70°C], these things are all gone," says Christopher Muller,

CAMPYLOBACTER

Campylobacter is a spiral-shaped bacteria, and there are a number of strains of it. The one that most commonly makes people sick is known as *Campylobacter jejuni*. This bacteria grows best at a bird's body temperature, and birds can carry it without becoming ill. Yet it can make humans quite sick. *Campylobacter* is not as well known as some other troublesome infectious agents, but it is responsible for sickening four times

A micrograph of *Campylobacter jejuni*, the bacteria that causes campylobacteriosis director, Center for Multi-Unit Restaurant Management at Orlando's University of Central Florida.

But it's not always that simple.

The real issue at restaurants is cross-contamination, says Marion Nestle, professor of nutrition at New York University and author of *What to Eat.*

"You have to hope that raw, contaminated chicken wasn't lying on the surface that the salad was cut on," she says.

While health codes generally require restaurant kitchens to have separate areas for handling meat and uncooked foods, many people cooking at home use wooden cutting boards to cut raw meat, then fail to wash them in hot water, notes Darra Goldstein, editor-in-chief at *Gastronomica*, a journal of food and culture.

The big restaurant chains insist their chicken is safe:

• KFC. "Properly cooked chicken is the best safeguard," says spokeswoman Laurie Schalow. "And our chicken is cooked at a high temperature using computerized controls that exceed all standards to ensure our chicken is safe to eat."

• Burger King. "We assure that all our chicken—and meat products—are properly and fully cooked," says spokeswoman Edna Johnson.

• Wendy's. Spokesman Denny Lynch was unable to reach food safety officials at the company late Monday, but he noted that the chain's chicken is frozen, not fresh, which, he says, can add a layer of protection for bacteria-related issues.

McDonald's did not immediately respond.

Muller, the professor, said Monday that the *Consumer Reports* study was not going to dissuade him from his dinner plans: to purchase a rotisserie chicken at his local Publix supermarket.

But he said, "I'm sorry you told me."

—*Bruce Horovitz*

as many people as *Salmonella.* Campylobacteriosis is the infectious disease caused by these bacteria. Most cases of campylobacteriosis occur in individuals and are not part of large outbreaks affecting many people.

Many cases of campylobacteriosis result from handling or eating raw or undercooked poultry and meat. Just a single drop of juice from raw chicken can infect someone.

Campylobacter is frequently spread during food preparation. This happens when someone cuts uncooked meat or poultry on a cutting board and then cuts fruits or vegetables on the same board without thoroughly washing it first. The same holds true for using the same cutting utensils without washing them. This is known as cross-contamination.

Campylobacter bacteria are also spread in unpasteurized milk and contaminated drinking water. Water from mountain streams or lakes near where cattle graze can become contaminated when cattle feces end up in the water. Water can also be contaminated by the feces of wild birds. Household pets can be infected as well, and at times, humans have become infected by coming in contact with the stools of a sick cat or dog.

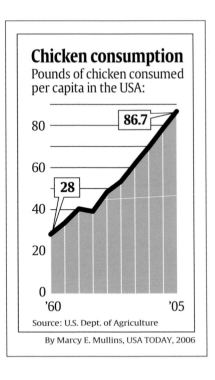

Chicken consumption
Pounds of chicken consumed per capita in the USA:

Source: U.S. Dept. of Agriculture

By Marcy E. Mullins, USA TODAY, 2006

Among the most common symptoms of campylobacteriosis are diarrhea, stomach cramps, and fever. At times, the diarrhea may be bloody and the stricken person may experience nausea and vomiting as well. The symptoms usually begin to surface from two to five days after the individual is exposed to the infectious agent. The illness lasts for about seven days.

DIAGNOSIS AND TREATMENT

The symptoms of many foodborne illnesses are similar to those of campylobacteriosis. Lab tests are necessary to determine which illness it is. Most cases of campylobacteriosis are not treated. Infected individuals endure the symptoms until the illness has finally run its course. Doctors usually suggest that people with campylobacteriosis drink lots of fluids while they have diarrhea. Doctors may prescribe antibiotics for the most severe cases.

Most people infected with campylobacteriosis are fine after their symptoms fade. A small number of people will develop arthritis. A smaller number of others will develop Guillain-Barré syndrome. With this disease, a person's immune system attacks the body's own nerve cells. It can make people so weak they need help to breathe. Most patients recover, though some continue to experience weakness. Guillain-Barré affects one to two people out of every one hundred thousand with campylobacteriosis. It has been estimated that campylobacteriosis leads to as many as 40 percent of the cases of Guillain-Barré syndrome in the United States.

NORWALK AND NOROVIRUSES

The Norwalk virus is a small, round virus that causes an illness that affects the stomach and intestines. Some people call this a stomach bug, or stomach flu, but it is not really flu. This category of virus also includes at least eleven other related viruses known as noroviruses.

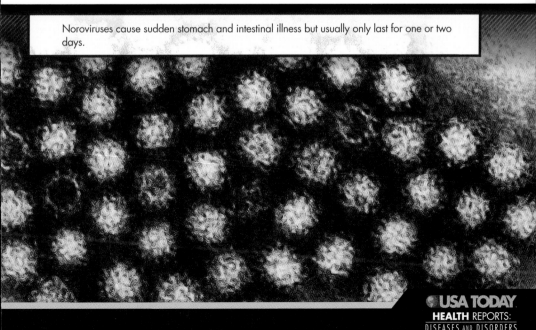

Noroviruses cause sudden stomach and intestinal illness but usually only last for one or two days.

www.usatoday.com

January 9, 2007

From the Pages of USA TODAY

'Stomach flu' rips through the nation;

That calamity in the gut is probably the work of nasty norovirus

Stomach viruses tearing through communities from California to the Carolinas wrecked the December holidays for some, and they are getting the new year off to an uncomfortable start for others.

The most likely culprits, experts say, are noroviruses, the most common cause of contagious gastroenteritis, better known as the "stomach flu." Cases occur every winter, but health officials say that in recent weeks they have seen two to three times as many cases as usual.

The virus, best known as the cause of cruise ship outbreaks, is easy to catch, hard to wipe out and seems to be everywhere at once.

Last week, San Quentin State Prison [in California] closed to new prisoners and visitors after nearly 500 inmates and guards fell ill with vomiting, diarrhea, stomach cramps, headaches

These viruses are extremely common throughout the country. It's been estimated that there are more than 180,000 cases of illness caused by these viruses each year in the United States. The viruses have also been linked to outbreaks of intestinal illness on cruise ships and in camps, schools, and families.

HOW ARE THESE VIRUSES SPREAD?

These viruses only exist in humans and cannot multiply outside the human body. Any of them may be present in the vomit or feces of an infected individual. It can remain in the ill person's feces for as long as two weeks after the individual feels better.

and low fever. Similar symptoms have been plaguing staff and residents of nursing homes in several states. College and pro athletes have missed games. Hundreds of patients have sought help in emergency rooms since mid-December. Nearly 400 people on a Caribbean cruise last month and 700 on a trans-Atlantic cruise in November were stricken, according to Associated Press reports.

Norovirus infection usually clears up after two or three days, but medical epidemiologist Marc-Alain Widdowson, a *Norovirus* expert at the Centers for Disease Control and Prevention, says the misery of those days shouldn't be dismissed.

"When you're ill, you're really ill," he says. "People (can) vomit 20 times a day."

Norovirus can be spread through contaminated food or water, causing large outbreaks. About half of foodborne diseases are thought to be caused by *Norovirus*, the CDC says.

But this winter, it is spreading mainly from person to person through communities, and experts believe the majority of cases are unreported.

Once it's in the house, experts say, it's tough to wipe out. It can linger for days on surfaces such as children's toys, keyboards, telephones and doorknobs, and both vomit and stool are highly infectious. It is present in the stool up to three weeks after the patient recovers, so health officials stress the importance of hand-washing, especially after using the bathroom and before preparing food.

The virus causes illness year-round, though like many, it is more common in colder months. Why it's so widespread this winter is not known, Widdowson says. "Some years, it does seem to be a lot worse than others, and this is one of those."

—Anita Manning

The viruses can be easily passed to others. If an ill person prepares food after going to the bathroom without washing his or her hands, anyone who eats that food can become ill. People can also become ill by drinking *Norovirus*-contaminated water or even by using ice made from it. Oysters and other shellfish from contaminated waters can transmit these viruses too.

The most common symptoms of these viruses are nausea, vomiting, and diarrhea. Some people also experience stomach cramps and muscle aches, and may have a low-grade fever and chills. Ill individuals have headaches and feel quite tired. Usually these viruses come on suddenly, quickly making the infected person very

Shellfish can transmit noroviruses if they came from contaminated waters.

ill. However, the symptoms generally do not last very long—usually only for a day or two.

DIAGNOSIS AND TREATMENT

Doctors have no routine tests to detect the noroviruses, so diagnosis can be difficult. A doctor usually makes a diagnosis based on the symptoms and the short time that the person is ill. Some new methods to detect these viruses have been developed. These tests can only be performed in specialized labs and involve using stool specimens or blood samples from the infected person. Such tests are usually reserved for a small number of cases associated with large-scale outbreaks. They are generally not available for testing in individual cases.

At present no antiviral medication is effective against these viruses, and the antibiotics used to treat bacteria do not work on viruses. Doctors recommend that people suffering from *Norovirus* infections rest and drink plenty of fluids to prevent dehydration.

Usually no long-term consequences result from these viruses. However, a person can be infected with noroviruses more than once. Since there are many different strains of noroviruses, having one type does not provide protection from infection with another strain.

The illnesses described in this chapter are among the most common foodborne diseases caused directly by bacteria and viruses. The more you know about them, the better able you will be to safeguard your own good health.

CHAPTER FOUR

THE TERRIBLE TOXINS — FOOD POISONING

Food poisoning is another kind of foodborne disease. In these cases, it is not the actual microbes in the food that cause people to become ill. The culprits are the toxins, or poisons, that these microbes produce. In some infections, microbes also produce toxins inside the infected person's body. In food-poisoning cases, the microbes produce toxins in the contaminated food, and when people eat the food, the toxins make them very ill.

These toxins are usually fast acting. If a person eats food containing a fairly large amount of a toxin, it is likely that he or she will be ill that day. In some cases, it can happen in minutes. It is important to know about food poisoning to stay healthy.

BOTULISM

Botulism is a rare but extremely serious form of food poisoning. It is caused by a toxin produced by the rod-shaped bacteria *Clostridium botulinum*. Probable incidents of botulism were recorded in Europe in earlier times. During an outbreak in Germany in 1735, a number of people died after eating contaminated sausage. The term *botulism* is taken from the Latin word *botulus* meaning "sausage." There are three main types of botulism, but the one discussed here is foodborne botulism.

The botulinal toxin produced in food is extremely toxic. It is about 100 million times more toxic than the venom of a cobra,

A micrograph of *Clostridium botulinum*, which causes botulism

© Richard Kessel & Gene Shih/Visuals Unlimited, Inc.

India's deadliest snake. One millionth of a gram of botulinal toxin is enough to kill a human. One pint (0.5 liter) of it could wipe out everyone on the planet.

SYMPTOMS

The first symptoms caused by the botulinal toxin include double vision, blurred vision, drooping eyelids, and slurred speech. The person will also usually experience dry mouth, trouble swallowing, and overall muscle weakness. Unless the stricken individual receives treatment soon, the situation worsens. The toxin is slowly absorbed by the intestines and then enters the bloodstream. It begins to attack the nervous system by binding to the nerve endings where the nerves join the muscles. This stops the nerves from signaling the muscles and results in paralysis of the arms, legs, torso, and respiratory (breathing) muscles. If a person can't breathe, he or she will die.

In most instances, the symptoms start between eighteen and thirty-six hours after eating contaminated food. However, symptoms can start as early as four hours after ingesting the toxin or as late as ten days afterward.

Botulism is an illness that often comes from eating improperly home-canned foods. That was the case with a Wisconsin woman who did a lot of home canning and entertaining. While preparing for a dinner party on the day she became ill, she decided to gather the foods she would need later that evening.

At first she thought that she would serve carrots and opened a jar of the ones she had canned. She dipped her pinkie finger into the jar and sampled the juice. But she thought the flavor was off and decided not to use them. She served her guests green beans instead.

The dinner party went well, but two days later, the hostess felt dizzy and found it hard to walk. She went to the hospital emergency room, where the staff thought that she might have had a stroke.

www.usatoday.com

USA TODAY

Life

SECTION D

July 27, 2009

From the Pages of USA TODAY

Safe canning requires rules

Recession gardens renew interest in preserving food

Staring at a backyard full of bounty and unsure what to do with all those green beans or tomatoes?

You have company, say experts in food preservation. Their phones are ringing constantly this summer with calls from novice or rusty gardeners who want to know how to safely can fruits and vegetables. (Vegetable seed sales were up by double digits this year, suppliers told USA TODAY recently.)

Some folks also want to preserve produce from local farms and farmers markets, the experts say.

"People are reaching out, wanting to preserve food for the first time or getting out equipment that hasn't been used in years," says Elizabeth Andress, director of the National Center for Home Food Preservation, based at the University of Georgia.

The recession, food safety concerns and the local food movement (given a boost by first gardener Michelle Obama) may be inspiring the trend.

Andress and other experts say they are happy to handle the calls and are setting up as many how-to workshops as possible, usually through state cooperative extension offices. They are more worried about self-made kitchen chemists who don't call.

"This is one area where you don't want to be Rachael Ray. You don't want to add your flair" to recipes and techniques backed by good science and rigorous testing, says Ben Chapman, a food safety specialist at North Carolina State University.

"Any modification could result in an unsafe product," says Angela Fraser, a food safety education specialist at Clemson

By then her speech was slurred and she was experiencing muscle weakness, so their suspicions were not unreasonable.

DIAGNOSIS

Luckily, one of the physicians thought of botulism and asked the woman if she had recently eaten anything that had not tasted quite

University in South Carolina.

It's also risky to rely on an index card Grandma used in 1954 or even a publication from the U.S. Department of Agriculture dated before 1994, says Luke LaBorde, associate professor of food science at Penn State University. Some techniques have changed, he says, to keep up with science.

The consequences for improper canning techniques can be serious, especially if consumers mishandle foods with low acid content, such as green beans and asparagus. Spores from the bacterium *Clostridium botulinum* may grow in such foods, creating toxins that can cause paralysis and death. In one recent case, reported in Spokane, Wash., a woman was put on a ventilator and two children were more mildly sickened after eating improperly canned green beans, Chapman says.

New canners are much less likely to get in trouble with high-acid foods, such as fruit preserves and pickles, Andress says. The canning process for such foods is simpler and requires just a basic boiling water canner. Low-acid foods must be processed in a pressure canner,

a more complicated piece of equipment requiring extra steps and precautions.

For folks who would rather not go to so much trouble, she says, there's freezing: It's simple, works well for many foods and, as long as your power supply is reliable, it's safe. Instructions on freezing and drying food are at the center website.

—Kim Painter

USA TODAY Snapshots®

Farmers markets cropping up

How the number of farmers markets in the USA has grown over the past 10 years:

2,410

4,385

Source: Northeast Midwest Institute, from U.S. Department of Agriculture data

By Mary Cadden and Robert W. Ahrens, USA TODAY, 2007

right. The woman remembered the carrots, but she was too weak to speak. She scribbled the word *carrots* on a piece of paper she had with her, and that made all the difference.

The jar of carrots in question was found at her home and tested. When a sample from the jar was given to a laboratory mouse, the animal was dead less than eight hours later. The same thing happened when a sample from the woman's blood was injected into another laboratory mouse.

The woman survived, but her recovery was not easy. She had to remain in the hospital on a respirator for over six months. The partial paralysis of her breathing muscles made it impossible for her to breathe without assistance. During that time, she had to be fed intravenously. Slow recoveries are not uncommon in cases of botulism. The person can only recover when the affected nerves grow new endings, and this can take months.

Over the months, the woman received intensive physical therapy, and in time, some of her muscle movement began to return. Getting back to normal felt like a daily challenge, yet this woman was lucky. Many times, botulism is fatal.

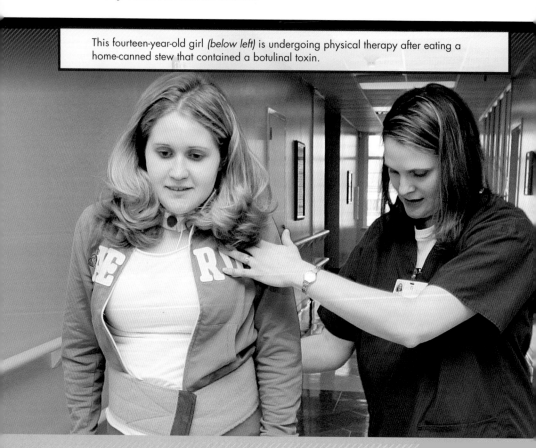

This fourteen-year-old girl *(below left)* is undergoing physical therapy after eating a home-canned stew that contained a botulinal toxin.

Put It on Your Face—Not on Your Plate

While the botulinal toxin causes a paralysis that can result in death, in recent years, there has been some good news about this toxin as well. Medical researchers have found ways that people can benefit from it. One way is to turn it into a medicine to control involuntary or unwanted muscle contractions.

Doctors inject a patient with very small amounts of a purified form of the toxin, when they want to interfere with a muscle's ability to contract. Botox, as this sterile form of the toxin is known, was the first approved in 1989 to treat two eye muscle disorders—one of which was uncontrollable blinking.

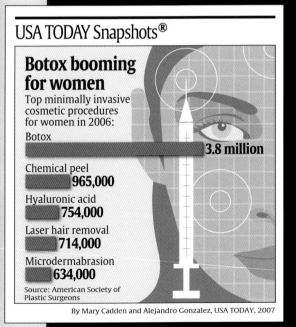

USA TODAY Snapshots®

Botox booming for women

Top minimally invasive cosmetic procedures for women in 2006:

Botox **3.8 million**

Chemical peel **965,000**

Hyaluronic acid **754,000**

Laser hair removal **714,000**

Microdermabrasion **634,000**

Source: American Society of Plastic Surgeons

By Mary Cadden and Alejandro Gonzalez, USA TODAY, 2007

In these cases, doctors saw that Botox had an unexpected beneficial side effect. It softened some of the lines around the eyes, making the patients look younger and less tired. This led to still another use of the toxin. In April 2002, Botox was approved to treat frown lines between the eyebrows. It has also been used to lessen the appearance of other facial lines.

The woman was also fortunate that the emergency room doctor had thought of botulism, since botulism has become fairly rare in the United States. Only about twenty to thirty cases of foodborne botulism are reported in the United States annually. Diagnosis is often difficult as botulism mimics aspects of other conditions. First, tests have to rule out these other diseases.

Testing for botulism usually involves live mice and is generally done at state health department laboratories and the Centers for Disease Control and Prevention. A small amount of the patient's blood or stool is injected into a mouse, and the animal is observed for signs of the illness. The bacteria that cause botulism can also be identified from the stool of an individual with foodborne botulism.

TREATMENT

The treatment for botulism varies depending on when an accurate diagnosis is made. If the condition is diagnosed early enough, the patient can be given an antitoxin to stop the toxin from circulating in the blood. An antitoxin is a substance used to neutralize the effects of the toxin or poison in the person's body. This prevents the person's condition from getting worse, but a botulism victim will still need time to recover from the damage already done. If the illness is diagnosed early enough, the doctor may try to remove what's left of the contaminated food from the patient's body through enemas or by induced vomiting. Although botulism can cause death due to respiratory failure, this has become less likely in the last fifty years. With the use of mechanical ventilators and other devices, the death rate from botulism has dropped from 50 percent to 8 percent.

Most cases of botulism in the United States come from improperly processed home-canned foods. The bacteria thrive in the food and produce the harmful toxin. People who do home canning should follow strict hygienic practices and process the food with the high heat of pressure canners.

A pressure canner is a metal kettle with a locked lid and a temperature gauge. It is especially designed for low-acid foods, such as red meat, seafood, poultry, and most fresh vegetables. These foods require a higher processing temperature to kill harmful bacteria. Health authorities further suggest that all home-canned foods be boiled for an additional twenty minutes before being eaten to be certain that they are safe.

STAPHYLOCOCCAL FOOD POISONING

Staphylococcal food poisoning is a gastrointestinal illness caused by the *Staphylococcus aureus* bacteria. The *Staphylococcus aureus* is a fairly common bacteria, but as the germ multiplies in food, it can produce seven different toxins that can result in food poisoning.

The bacteria get into the food through food handlers who have infected eyes, fingers, rashes, or nasal secretions. While infected food handlers tend to be the main source of the problem, equipment and cutting surfaces have also been sources of contamination. The foods most likely to be contaminated are those that do not require cooking but do involve a good deal of handling. These would include sliced meat platters, sandwiches, and salads where a number of ingredients are handled and combined.

A micrograph of *Staphylococcus aureus*, which causes Staphylococcal food poisoning

October 24, 1989

From the Pages of USA TODAY

FDA bans import of Chinese mushrooms

The Food and Drug Administration issued a ban Monday on all mushrooms imported from China. The reason: Repeated findings of a bacteria-produced toxin that can cause severe food poisoning.

In May, the FDA banned Chinese mushrooms shipped in institutional-size cans (No. 10 can size, 68 oz. [2 kg] drained weight) because of food-poisoning outbreaks involving 100 people, 16 of them hospitalized. There have been no known deaths, says the FDA's Chris Lecos.

Since then, the toxin has been discovered in other size containers as well, prompting the agency to extend the ban.

About half of all mushrooms shipped to the USA come from China; two-thirds of the mushrooms China ships here are the institutional size, Lecos says.

"There's still the possibility that some of these products may be on people's shelves," he says. Any mushrooms from the People's Republic of China should not be used; return them to the store where purchased, Lecos says.

The poison, staphylococcal enterotoxin, is produced by *Staphylococcus aurea* bacteria. It can cause nausea, vomiting and abdominal cramps

lasting two or three days.

Tests suggest the contamination is from mishandling before and during canning, Lecos says.

Because contamination may be widespread throughout the Chinese mushroom industry, the FDA will detain all shipments indefinitely until satisfied the appropriate sanitation measures are taken, he says.

—Dan Sperling

Refused entry

Almost 900 imports of food and vitamins from China were refused entry to the USA by the Food and Drug Administration from May 2006 through April. Types of items with most refusals:

Fish/seafood
340

Vegetable/products
145

Vitamins/minerals
142

Fruit/products
85

Bean curd/sauces
51

Note: Products with most refusals may not be riskier because amounts imported are unknown.

Source: FDA   By Karl Gelles, USA TODAY, 2007

It is important to prevent the contamination of food with *Staphylococcus* before the toxin can be produced. The Centers for Disease Control and Prevention suggests the following measures to help stop staphylococcal food poisoning:

- Wash hands and under fingernails vigorously with soap and water before handling and preparing food.
- Do not prepare food if you are sneezing a lot due to a cold or have an eye infection.
- Do not prepare or serve food to others if you have wounds or skin infections on your hands or wrists.
- Keep kitchens and food-serving areas clean and sanitized.

SYMPTOMS AND TREATMENT

Staphylococcal food poisoning comes on fairly quickly. Sometimes symptoms will begin within thirty minutes. More commonly, they appear within one to six hours after the toxin has been ingested. The most common symptoms include nausea, vomiting, stomach cramps, and diarrhea, but no fever.

In most cases, the illness is fairly brief. While sick, people should rest and drink plenty of fluids. For some people, often the very young and the elderly, reactions to the toxin may be more severe because their immune systems are weaker. These people may require hospitalization and be given intravenous fluids.

CLOSTRIDIUM PERFRINGENS

Clostridium perfringens are another group of bacteria that produce a toxin that makes people sick. These rod-shaped bacteria are widely present in the environment. They are found in soil, the intestines of human and animals, dust, insects, and sewage.

Perfringens food poisoning is the illness caused by the toxin

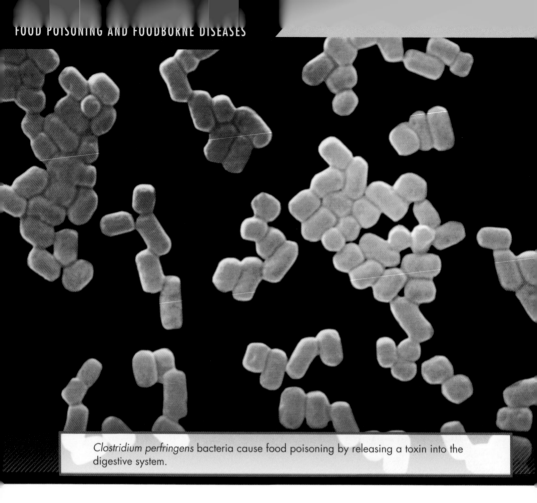

Clostridium perfringens bacteria cause food poisoning by releasing a toxin into the digestive system.

produced by these bacteria. At times, it has even been called the food service germ. That is because these food poisoning outbreaks often occur at schools, prisons, camps, hospitals, and nursing homes.

In most cases, poor temperature control has been a factor. Even after food is cooked, small numbers of these organisms can still be present in it. When food is kept at temperatures between 70 and 140°F (21 to 60°C) and the air and moisture levels are right, these organisms will produce the toxin that causes the illness. This sometimes happens in cafeteria-style settings where large amounts of food are prepared several hours before serving.

In many cases, this has led to large numbers of people getting sick at one time. It might be dozens of children who ate at an outdoor camp cookout or everyone who ate a particular dish at a church supper served buffet-style. Meat, poultry, cooked dried beans—such as refried beans—and gravies are among the most common sources of the bacteria.

One outbreak occurred among factory workers at a company banquet in Connecticut. A lovely buffet was served, but more than five hundred people became ill after eating the food. An analysis of the food showed that the gravy was the problem. It had been made twelve to twenty-four hours earlier and had been left out for too long. Although it was reheated shortly before being served, the length of time it was reheated and the temperature weren't enough to make the gravy safe to eat.

SYMPTOMS

The main symptoms of perfringens food poisoning are diarrhea and stomach cramps that frequently begin between eight and twenty-two hours after the toxin has been ingested. In most cases, the illness is over in twenty-four hours, and as a result, people call it the "24-hour flu." There is actually no such thing. These cases are just mild forms of food poisoning.

Perfringens food poisoning is one of the most commonly reported foodborne illnesses. The Centers for Disease Control and Prevention estimates that as many as ten thousand people a year in the United States get this illness. Beyond this, large numbers of cases are never reported because people recover so rapidly. This illness is most serious for the very young and the very old.

CHAPTER FIVE

PARASITES — UNWANTED GUESTS

I t was spring 1993 in Milwaukee, Wisconsin, and for a little while, some residents felt as if their city was under siege. Instead of going out to stores or sporting events, a large number of city residents were remaining at home close to their bathrooms. At first, people did not know what was happening, but the problem soon became public knowledge. Hundreds of thousands of Milwaukeeans had diarrhea.

The problem only lasted about two weeks, yet it certainly took its toll on Milwaukee's population. In fact, by the time it was over, the official tolls were staggering. About 403,000 residents had become ill, which resulted in forty-four thousand doctor visits and 725,000 lost work or school days.

Those very large numbers were caused by a very tiny parasite. A parasite is a plant or animal that lives off a host and can pose a health threat. The parasite that had gotten into the city's water supply was a microscopic menace called *Cryptosporidium parvum*, commonly known as crypto. When crypto entered Milwaukee's water supply, the city made public health history for all the wrong reasons. It became the site of the largest waterborne disease outbreak in a modern nation.

Since then crypto has been recognized as one of the most common causes of waterborne diseases in the United States. It lives in the intestines of animals and people and is passed in the stool. According to the Centers for Disease Control and Prevention, this parasite may sometimes get into the drinking and recreational waters in the United States as well as throughout much of the world.

Crypto parasites spread easily. Millions of these may be released in a single bowel movement from just one infected person or animal.

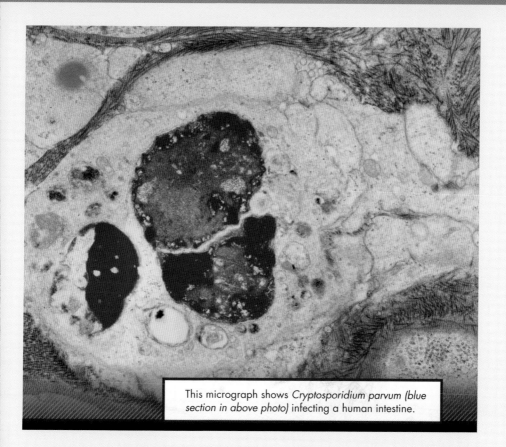

This micrograph shows *Cryptosporidium parvum (blue section in above photo)* infecting a human intestine.

Therefore, the parasite may be present in the soil, in the food, in the water, or on any surface that could have been contaminated by infected human or animal feces. When a person unknowingly swallows the microscopic parasite, he or she becomes infected as well.

SYMPTOMS

The symptoms of cryptosporidiosis, the illness caused by the parasite, usually appear between two and ten days after the person has become infected. The most common symptom of the illness is watery diarrhea. Other symptoms are dehydration, weight loss, stomach cramps, fever, nausea, and vomiting. In a healthy person with a strong immune system, the symptoms usually last between one and two weeks. For some people, the symptoms seem to run in

www.usatoday.com

News

SECTION A

October 21, 1998

From the Pages of USA TODAY

Studies suggest millions of Americans could get sick each year

SPECIAL REPORT: DRINKING WATER'S HIDDEN DANGERS

There's no telling precisely how many Americans get sick each year from drinking bad water. But it's safe to say there are a lot more of them than anyone knows about.

From 1993 to 1996, the most recent years for which the Centers for Disease Control and Prevention (CDC) has records, there were 52 confirmed outbreaks of waterborne illness that sickened 408,000 people and killed 111. All the deaths and 403,000 of the illnesses were linked to a 1993 bad water outbreak in Milwaukee.

Researchers say those numbers barely scratch the surface of what's really going on. "I would say the cases we learn about are the tip of the iceberg," says Deborah Levy, a waterborne-disease expert at the CDC.

There's no suggestion that the United States is returning to an era when waterborne plagues such as cholera and typhoid were leading causes of death. Today's drinking water problems are far more likely to cause nausea and diarrhea than any mortal epidemic.

But gastrointestinal illnesses from bad

cycles. A person will begin to feel better, only to feel sick again a few days later until the illness is finally over.

Anyone can get cryptosporidiosis, but some people are at higher risk. These include very young children and pregnant women. They can be more susceptible to dehydration. People who have severely weakened immune systems also can become seriously ill. This includes those with HIV (human immunodeficiency virus)/AIDS (acquired immunodeficiency syndrome), cancer patients on chemotherapy, and people with various inherited diseases that weaken their immune system. Individuals who have received a recent organ or bone marrow transplant are at high risk as well.

water have become increasingly common, according to academic and government studies. The illnesses pose what many researchers see as a serious public health threat with life-threatening consequences, particularly to people in weakened medical condition.

Waterborne illness "is not simply the concern of past generations, (it) must remain on the current public health agenda," Morris and Levin wrote in a 1995 study. But "addressing (those) concerns . . . will require more reliable data."

Even getting a handle on illness . . . such as *Cryptosporidium*, the bug behind the Milwaukee outbreak, is a daunting task.

The problem is that people tend to attribute stomach problems to flus or food poisoning. They let them run their course over a few days and rarely see a doctor. Even if they do get help, doctors rarely do the kinds of tests that can peg bad water as the culprit.

In the rare cases when doctors find bad water is behind an illness, there generally is no requirement that they report it.

"Nobody really has any idea of how many people are getting sick and dying," says Rebecca Calderon, a waterborne-disease expert at the EPA [Environmental Protection Agency].

The medical community is especially concerned by the threat that *Cryptosporidium* and other bacteria pose to the rising number of people with weak immune systems, such as cancer patients getting chemotherapy, organ transplant recipients and AIDS patients. The elderly, pregnant women and infants also face greater risks from bad water.

For five years, the CDC has maintained a standing recommendation that Americans with those conditions should consider boiling their water before drinking it, regardless of its source.

—*Peter Eisler*

Crypto is an extremely difficult parasite to conquer. This is partly because it has a hard outer shell protecting it. Its outer coating makes this parasite especially resistant to chlorine-based water purifiers. Crypto has been known to survive for long periods in swimming pools that were clean and had the proper chlorine levels. Swimmers who accidentally swallow some of this pool water can become infected. This parasite can also be present in lakes, rivers, streams, and ponds that may be contaminated with sewage or feces from either humans or animals. Crypto can survive in both hot and cold water, in freshwater and in salt water.

At times, farm animals, such as cows and pigs, can cause a problem

in some areas. A single dairy cow produces about 120 pounds [54 kg] of wet manure a day. That's equal to the daily waste from twenty to forty humans. If not correctly managed and disposed of, farm animal waste can pollute the environment. Improperly used or stored waste can contaminate rivers and underground drinking water supplies.

When crypto got into Milwaukee's water supply, it caused havoc in the community because so many people became ill during the outbreak. Once inside the body, the parasite's hard outer shell breaks open, allowing the parasite to multiply in the intestines. Thousands of people in Milwaukee were hospitalized and more than one hundred people died.

Who Is Most at Risk for Cryptosporidiosis?

According to the Centers for Disease Control and Prevention, the people most likely to become infected with crypto include:

- Children who attend day care centers, including diaper-aged children
- Child care workers
- Parents of infected children
- International travelers
- Backpackers, hikers, and campers who drink unfiltered, untreated water
- Swimmers who swallow water while swimming in swimming pools, lakes, rivers, ponds, and streams
- People who drink from shallow, unprotected wells

TREATMENT

Many of those who died were AIDS patients whose fragile immune systems were no match for the parasite. Others who died were battling cancer as well. One woman with a severe case of cryptosporidiosis lost her spleen as a result of the illness. Another patient went into kidney failure and needed dialysis before receiving a kidney transplant the following year.

Yet for most people with healthy immune systems, the illness soon passed. But people's doubts and fears tended to linger. They had heard the expression, "Don't drink the water," when it came to traveling in an underdeveloped country, but they couldn't believe that the water in a modern city in the United States could make people sick. Milwaukee wasn't the only place where this happened. That same year, crypto also invaded the water systems in New York; Washington, D.C.; and suburban Virginia. The following year, crypto claimed thirty-nine lives in an outbreak in Las Vegas, Nevada.

WHAT HAPPENED TO MILWAUKEE'S WATER?

As might be expected, crypto entered Milwaukee's water supply by mistake. Since chlorination can't kill this parasite, it must be filtered out of untreated water along with other impurities. At the time of the outbreak, the city had been trying a new chemical filter to do this at one of its water purification plants. A water filter traps large contaminants from passing through the water. Most modern filters also use chemical processes to filter the water. The chemicals separate the contaminants from the drinking water supply.

There had been signs early on that the new chemical was not all that Milwaukee city officials had hoped it would be. Complaints from city residents had flowed into the water department like water from the tap. People said that their water looked cloudy and smelled

The Howard Avenue water treatment plant was the source of the 1993 crypto outbreak in Milwaukee, Wisconsin.

bad. Not realizing that the new chemical simply wasn't up to the job, water department officials added more of it to the water supply, hoping to remedy the problem.

At about the same time, city officials learned that waste from a slaughterhouse had been illegally flowing directly into the water system. To make matters worse, the weather had been unusual that year. There had been a very wet spring, causing lots of runoff water to flow into the streams flowing into Lake Michigan—the source of Milwaukee's water. By the first week in April, everything seemed to have come together in the worst way possible. Lots of people were getting sick. Doctors' offices and hospitals were soon filled with new cases. In some areas, it was hard to care for everyone because so many of the nurses and other medical staff were sick as well.

Another Microscopic Menace

*C*yclospora cayetanensis, like crypto, is a tiny one-celled parasite that can make you sick. *Cyclospora* is also spread through food or water that has been contaminated by feces containing the parasite. The earliest known cases of *Cyclospora* infection occurred in 1979. Cases were reported more frequently in the 1980s. Since that time, numerous outbreaks have occurred in both the United States and Canada.

Symptoms begin to appear about a week after the person has become infected. There is usually watery diarrhea, loss of appetite, weight loss, stomach cramps, nausea, increased gas, muscle aches, low-grade fever, and exhaustion.

If not treated, the infection can last anywhere from a few days to a few months. The usual treatment for this illness is a combination of two antibiotics. Anyone who thinks that he or she may be infected with *Cyclospora* should see a physician.

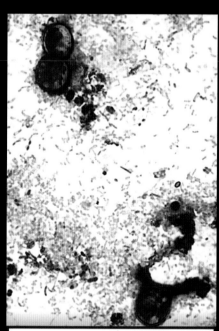

The red dots in the micrograph above are *Cyclospora cayetanensis*.

HOW THE CITY REACTED

Crypto is diagnosed through special laboratory tests performed on stool samples, and as these tests were completed throughout the city, the results were clear—crypto was in the water system. The city sprang into action to correct matters. Through the media, the message went out to all Milwaukee residents—as well as to the people living in the ten suburbs that use city water—to boil their drinking water until further notice.

Meanwhile, the city began revamping its water treatment system. It installed a new water intake pipe that extended farther into Lake Michigan to reach a purer water source. Milwaukee added enhanced filters and monitoring devices to the system as well. The city installed heightened security measures at the city's two water plants, and health officials began to track more carefully any signs of an illness outbreak. While Milwaukee city officials wished that the crypto outbreak had never occurred, they were pleased with the changes they made to ensure that it never happens again.

PARASITIC WORMS

People can become infected with other parasites as well. Among these are several different types of tapeworms, which include the beef tapeworm (*Taenia saginata*) and the pork tapeworm (*Taenia solium*). Cattle and pigs can pick up these parasites by eating an infected flea. Humans become infected when they eat poorly cooked or raw beef or pork that contains tapeworm eggs or larvae (the immature form of the tapeworm). The larvae of this parasitic organism finds its way to the intestines, where it matures into an adult tapeworm. If not diagnosed and treated, the tapeworm can live in the body for years and grow as long as 20 to 30 feet (6 to 9 meters). Often the infected people have no symptoms and do not even know that they are infected, until they notice tapeworm segments that have passed from their bodies in their stool. Some infected individuals experience stomach pains, nausea, diarrhea, loss of appetite, and weight loss.

These ribbon-shaped worms are made up of segments. Each segment can produce eggs, which hatch into larvae. The beef tapeworm larvae remain in the intestine, where they are fairly harmless. However, the pork tapeworm larvae can travel through the tissues to other parts of the infected person's body, such as the liver, the lungs, and the central nervous system. The larvae develop into lesions or cysts, a condition known as cysticercosis. The cysts continue to grow and can stop the organ from functioning properly.

Adult tapeworms live in the small intestines of their hosts and can grow up to 30 feet (9 m) long. This is a beef tapeworm.

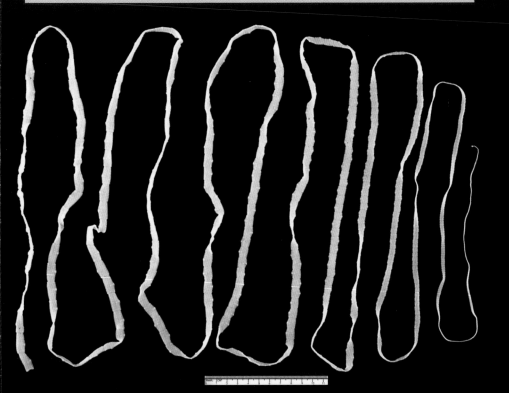

www.usatoday.com

USA TODAY

Life
SECTION D

October 6, 1997

From the Pages of USA TODAY

New microbes becoming global health risks

Emerging diseases, from neurocysticercosis, a brain infection caused by a parasite in undercooked pork, to *Mycoplasma pneumoniae*, an often overlooked cause of serious lung infection, are becoming more common in Americans' lives, scientists say.

The increasing reports of illness, many of them caused by food-borne bugs, are in part a result of global food distribution, which allows unusual microbes to ride into the USA on fresh produce, and of better technology, which allows doctors to identify disease-causing organisms, scientists reported at the Interscience Conference on Antimicrobial Agents and Chemotherapy. Some microbes are newly recognized, such as:

Cyclospora, the diarrhea-causing parasite that has made about 1,400 Americans sick this year and last. Most cases have been associated with eating

When the larvae infect the central nervous system, cysts may form in the brain as well as in the meninges (the tissues covering the brain). This is called neurocysticercosis. The brain cysts can result in headaches, confusion, seizures, meningitis, or dementia. In very severe cases, the patient may die.

TREATMENT

Tapeworm infection is most easily and successfully treated in the intestine, where oral medications can kill the adult tapeworm. Treatment becomes more difficult if the tapeworm has migrated to other areas of the body. In some cases, surgery is necessary to remove large cysts. In the worst cases, an organ transplant may be necessary.

raspberries imported from Guatemala, but this year cases have also been linked to lettuce and basil. The country of origin of these items hasn't been discovered, Relman says. The organism can be killed by cooking, but washing alone, even in bleach, doesn't appear to be effective. One option under consideration is irradiation, he says.

"Worms on the brain," the vivid name for infection with *Taenia solium*, a pig tapeworm that causes neurocysticercosis in humans, a rarely fatal brain disease characterized by seizures. "It's a very common infection in developing countries where pigs run free as scavengers and eat human feces," says Peter Schantz of the Centers for Disease Control and Prevention. The parasite is passed to humans in undercooked pork. "In the U.S., we don't get it because pigs are raised in controlled, hygienic conditions," he

says. But it does affect an estimated 1,000 people a year who come here from other countries, and those carrying the parasite in its larval stages, particularly food handlers and child-care workers, could pass it to others.

North American liver fluke, a fish parasite, sickened 19 people on a fishing trip north of Montreal [Quebec, Canada] two years ago, says J. Dick MacLean of McGill University Center for Tropical Diseases, Quebec. The parasite has been around a long time, he says, but had not been known to make people sick until that outbreak, in which people got abdominal pain and fever after eating raw fish they caught in a river. "It's one of several worms found in fish in North America," he says. "All fish should be frozen before it's eaten raw. Freezing will kill worms."

—Anita Manning

Tapeworm infection is not common in industrialized nations. It is much more of a problem in developing countries, where sanitation practices are often lax. With increased travel to these areas in recent years, more Americans have become infected.

While tapeworm is not common in humans in the United States, it is in dogs. Dogs can get it by eating an infected flea. They can also get it from eating animals outside such as mice and rabbits that are carrying the parasite. If your dog becomes infected with tapeworm, take your pet to a veterinarian for treatment. It's rare for humans to get tapeworms from their pets. A person would have had to accidentally swallow an infected flea that was on the pet. Most reported cases have involved very young children.

CHAPTER SIX

PRIONS

Alison Williams, a twenty-year-old from a coastal village in northern Wales in Great Britain, enjoyed being outdoors. She spent much of her spare time swimming and sailing in the beautiful mountain lakes near her home and loved every minute of it. Yet Alison was interested in more than just sports. She was a business student who hoped to one day enter the corporate world. With her keen intellect and outgoing personality, everyone who knew her felt that Alison had a bright future ahead.

But as it turned out, Alison had a very limited future. By the time she turned twenty-two, she had changed. The young woman who once loved being around people had become increasingly withdrawn. She seemed to have lost interest in people and in all the other things that used to be important to her. Alison quit school, even though she'd done well there, and moved back in with her parents and brother. Though she still liked the outdoors, she began spending a good deal of time alone in her bedroom. Some days she would sit on her bed for hours and stare blankly out the window.

Alison's parents took her to doctors to see what was happening to their daughter, but while something was obviously wrong, no one was quite sure what that was. She was later diagnosed as having some psychiatric problems. But as time passed, Alison's symptoms started becoming physical as well. Within three years, Alison had become incontinent (unable to control her bladder) and quite weak. It was not too long afterward that she died. Her father reported that in the month prior to her death, Alison had gone blind and lost the use of her tongue. He added that his daughter spent the last five months of her life in a coma.

Alison was not the only person in Great Britain to die after experiencing these strange symptoms. Zoe Jeffries, a vibrant, friendly young teen from Lancashire (a county in northwestern England), had also been a popular girl who loved sports. Zoe was what some people call a natural—she always did well at everything she tried. She won medals in dance competitions and was an outstanding gymnast. When she was just nine, she joined her school's drama club and often played the lead roles in school productions.

Yet her mother said that one day her daughter suddenly changed. Zoe didn't seem to want to do anything and spent most days crying. At times, she would scream for no apparent reason and refuse to leave the house. Zoe's father had recently died after a heart attack, so at first, her doctors thought that the young teen was just having a hard time adjusting to his death. She was given antidepressants, but like Alison, she did not get better.

Instead, her condition worsened. As the months passed, Zoe's mother noticed that her daughter wasn't walking properly. Zoe would hold her arms out while dragging one foot from behind. It was obvious that Zoe was having a hard time keeping her balance. Zoe's illness continued to get worse for two years. At the end of her life, she was nearly completely immobile. She was also unable to talk, feed herself, or control her bowels. Zoe died just one month before her fifteenth birthday.

MAD COW DISEASE

Alison and Zoe, along with others in Great Britain, died of an illness known as variant Creutzfeldt-Jakob disease (vCJD). You may know of this disease—it is more commonly known as mad cow disease.

The scientific name for mad cow disease in cows is bovine spongiform encephalopathy (BSE). The disease affects the cow's nervous system. Usually the animal will lose weight, have difficulty

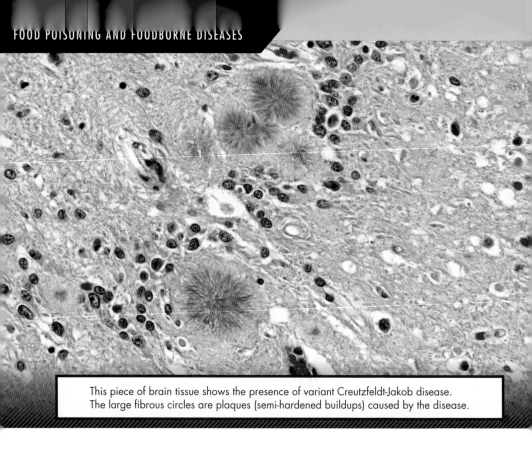

This piece of brain tissue shows the presence of variant Creutzfeldt-Jakob disease. The large fibrous circles are plaques (semi-hardened buildups) caused by the disease.

keeping its balance, and drool. At times it may weave its head, arch its back, and act as if it were crazy—hence the name mad cow disease. The problem is not due to bacteria or a virus, but instead, it is the result of prions, or defective proteins, that cause infectious diseases. In this case, the prions bond with the infected cow's brain cells. Scientists think that the prions alter the composition of the animal's brain cells, which eventually leads to its death.

Mad cow disease is believed to be transmitted when cattle eat these infectious prions. The prions, which cause BSE in an infected cow, reside in the cow's central nervous system—the brain, the spinal cord, and other nervous system tissue. At that time, the British routinely added the central nervous system tissue of slaughtered cows to the feed that was fed to cattle herds throughout the country. As the remains of infected cows became part of the mix, the disease was spread to more and more cows.

The cattle feed and live cattle were sold to other countries, and mad cow disease began to surface in different nations. Before long, small numbers of cases were reported in cattle in France, Ireland, the Netherlands, Portugal, and Switzerland. Cases of BSE also occurred in Canada, Denmark, the Falkland Islands, Germany, and Italy. All these infected cattle had been imported from Great Britain.

The problem spread to people, when they ate beef containing prions. People began falling victim to a devastating incurable brain disease linked to BSE, variant Creutzfeldt-Jakob disease. First, the victim exhibits signs of a personality change—often the person becomes depressed and withdrawn. As the disease progresses, it cripples the brain and weakens the body until the person dies.

FIGHTING BACK

In 1989 the British government took steps to stop what might have turned into an even more widespread health problem. It banned using cattle parts in cattle feed. The U.S. government also took measures to protect the beef supply. It banned all materials from cattle feed that might contain prions. That meant that the feed could no longer contain any ground-up cattle remains.

In addition, the U.S. Department of Agriculture began a more careful system of checking the cattle going to slaughter. As of March 2006,

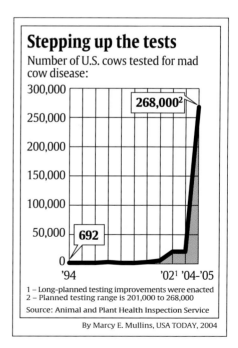

Stepping up the tests

Number of U.S. cows tested for mad cow disease:

268,000[2]

692

'94   '02[1] '04-'05

1 – Long-planned testing improvements were enacted
2 – Planned testing range is 201,000 to 268,000

Source: Animal and Plant Health Inspection Service

By Marcy E. Mullins, USA TODAY, 2004

December 30, 2003

From the Pages of USA TODAY

Genetically engineered cattle could resist mad cow disease; Animals not bred for consumption

Scientists at a South Dakota biotech company have genetically engineered cattle that appear to be resistant to mad cow disease, a paper published in the Monday issue of the journal *Nature Biotechnology* reports.

Although similar genetic engineering had been done in mice, this is the first time it has been accomplished in cattle.

The team of scientists first genetically engineered a line of cells in which the gene that produces the infectious proteins of mad cow disease—prions—was disabled. They then used those cells to clone 12 bulls so they were prevented from making the protein that, when "misfolded," causes prion diseases such as mad cow.

Those 12 bulls are now 2 years old and appear to be perfectly normal, says James Robl, president of Hematech Inc. in Sioux Falls, S.D., a biotech firm owned by the pharmaceutical division of Japanese brewing giant Kirin.

only three cows in the United States have been infected with BSE. Since this meat never entered the marketplace, the public was not endangered. There was also no concern about milk contamination, as it has been shown that BSE cannot be transmitted in cow's milk, even if the cow has BSE.

Yet are we really safe? Have we seen the last of mad cow disease? Some people think that there still isn't enough known about the disease to be sure. Some medical researchers believe that large numbers of people may already be infected with variant Creutzfeldt-Jakob disease and not know it, because diseases of

Although misfolded prions are not alive in the conventional sense, they can cause other proteins they come in contact with to misfold as well, creating the holes in the brain that characterize bovine spongiform encephalopathy (BSE, or spongy brain disease) in cattle and variant Creutzfeldt-Jakob disease in humans and other mammals.

When scientists took brain cells from the resistant cattle and mixed them with prions in a test tube, the brain cells did not misfold. Brain cells from normal cattle did. "That's a pretty good indication that they will not be able to contract the disease, nor would they be able to pass the disease on," Robl says.

Researchers injected mad cow-infected brain cells into the brains of some of the resistant cattle to see whether they develop the disease.

"In 1½ years we'll have an answer," because prion diseases are so slow to develop, says Jurgen Richt, a co-author on the paper and veterinary microbiologist at the National Animal Disease Center in Ames, Iowa.

The bulls appear to be developmentally and reproductively normal and should be able to breed true, creating a line of mad cow-resistant cattle, Robl says. Because they are still adolescents, they have not yet been bred, but their semen appears to be normal.

The cattle are not meant for human consumption, Robl says. If they prove incapable of getting mad cow disease, they could be used to produce products important to industry, such as blood serum used in making pharmaceuticals and collagen for cosmetics. George Seidel, a reproduction technologies expert at Colorado State University in Fort Collins, calls the research "elegant," but with mad cow disease so rare in North America, it's more a niche market: "There are much easier ways . . . than to make transgenic cattle."

—Elizabeth Weise

this type can have a very long incubation. The incubation period is the time it takes for symptoms to appear after ingesting the contaminated food.

KURU

Researchers report that kuru, another prion disease, can incubate for fifty years or longer in some people. It can remain dormant for years, only to flare up suddenly, resulting in dementia and death for its victim.

www.usatoday.com

USA TODAY

News
SECTION A

December 30, 2003

From the Pages of USA TODAY

Infected cow's age suggests lower risk

Animal was old enough that it could have eaten tainted feed before ban took effect in '97

The Washington state cow infected with mad cow disease was born four months before the United States and Canada instituted bans on feed containing potentially infectious material, U.S. Department of Agriculture [USDA] officials said Monday. The determination that the cow was more than 6½ years old—not 4½, as originally thought—is good news for the U.S. meat industry.

Feed that included cooked, ground-up cattle parts was legal in both the USA and Canada until August 1997. Ron DeHaven, USDA's chief veterinarian, said research has shown that eating this kind of feed is "the primary, if not the only way" the disease is spread from animal to animal.

The infection of a 4½-year-old cow would indicate that the feed ban wasn't working, but an older cow could have eaten infected feed.

This means that while there might be stray cases of mad cow disease from the use of infected feed in the late 1990s, it is likely that very few of those animals are still alive because most U.S. beef cattle are slaughtered at 18–24 months old. The only cattle likely to have been alive prior to the feed ban would be the smaller number of dairy cattle and breeding bulls prized for milk output or excellent genes. Such animals are allowed to live as long as 10–15 years, said Deb Roeber, a beef specialist at the University of Minnesota.

Mad cow disease, or bovine spongiform encephalopathy, is a concern because humans who eat tainted tissue can get a brain-wasting illness, variant Creutzfeldt-Jakob disease. Officials have said, however, that potentially infectious tissue from the infected cow's brain, spinal cord and nervous system was removed at slaughter.

A recall of 10,415 pounds [4,724 kg] of meat produced at Vern's Moses Lake Meats in Moses Lake, Wash., on Dec. 9— the day the infected cow was slaughtered there—is going well, said Ken Petersen of the USDA's Food Safety Inspection Service. More than 80% of the meat went to Washington and Oregon, and all major retailers that received it have been notified and have notified customers.

The recall has been extended to Alaska, California, Hawaii, Idaho, Montana, Nevada and Guam. But Petersen said that in each of those areas, there may be as few as one retail outlet affected.

—Elizabeth Weise

These researchers largely based their conclusions on work done with the native Fore group in Papua New Guinea, an island nation in the South Pacific Ocean. At one time, this group engaged in cannibalism. They honored their dead by cutting off parts of their bodies at funeral feasts and eating their flesh. They also unknowingly spread the disease by cutting off pieces of their deceased loved ones' brain tissue and rubbing these pieces against open cuts and scratches.

During the 1920s, thousands of these Fore died of kuru. The numbers only began to decrease after the Australian authorities outlawed the cannibalistic practices. At first, the tribe was reluctant to give up this custom, but by 1960, cannibalism had completely died out.

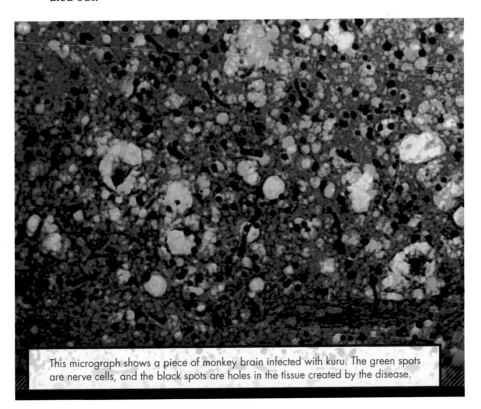

This micrograph shows a piece of monkey brain infected with kuru. The green spots are nerve cells, and the black spots are holes in the tissue created by the disease.

Kuru and Cannibalism—the Inside Scoop

After arriving in Papua New Guinea in the 1950s, Dr. Carleton Gajdusek *(below)*, an American pediatrician and virologist (scientist who studies viruses) from the National Institutes of Health, noticed a strange neurological disease affecting the Fore people. The illness was fatal and seemed to largely strike the tribe's women and children. The Fore named this illness kuru, which in their language meant "shaking disease." The illness took about a year and a half to run its course, and its symptoms were shaking, poor balance, slurred speech, coma, and death.

The Fore thought that kuru was the result of a curse on them. Gajdusek, after observation, felt certain that it was related to the Fore's eating habits. The mainstays of the tribe's diet were beans and sweet potatoes. The men hunted and ate the small game they caught. They didn't share it with the women and children. The women and children had to look for another source of protein. They found it in the funeral feasts held to honor their loved ones. There, the women would cut off and eat parts of people who had passed on. To them it was a way to keep those they cared about close to them. They did not eat people who died from leprosy or other diseases, but the bodies of those who died of kuru were considered clean and fit to eat. That was how the disease spread. Ironically, it was kept alive by those who died.

Dr. Carleton Gajdusek

Yet in chronicling the deaths of Fore people who died between 1996 and 2004, the researchers found that some of them still died of kuru. It was proof that this prion disease could lie silently in the bodies of some people for decades. If this was true for one prion disease, it could be true for another. People who ate infected beef before all the precautions against mad cow disease were put into place may show symptoms at any time. Some experts stress that in the years prior to the 1980s, British feed as well as cows were exported to many different countries around the globe—so no one can be sure where a mad cow disease outbreak may strike.

Not all scientists believe that vCJD will be much of a threat in the future. Some researchers point out that kuru is a human disease and is therefore more effective at infecting humans than mad cow disease could be. They also stress that the Fore either ate brain matter or rubbed it into their skin cuts, while beef eaters eat meat— which contains an extremely small amount of prions.

These scientists think that mad cow disease is likely to die out in a little over a decade because of all the measures taken to curtail it. So have we just about seen the last of mad cow disease, or are the worst outbreaks yet to come? Only time will tell.

CHAPTER SEVEN

KEEPING OUR FOOD SAFE

The United States has been concerned with food safety throughout much of its history. Yet when the nation was young, things were much different than they are in the twenty-first century. American pioneer and farm families did not have the luxury of supermarkets to shop in and restaurants to dine at. They grew most of what they ate.

Families had gardens and raised potatoes, tomatoes, corn, pumpkins, beans, and other vegetables. Young people were often sent into nearby wooded areas to gather berries and nuts for the family. The meat supply mainly came from the deer, wild turkeys, and quail the men hunted. Many families raised pigs and chickens on their farms as well. Food did not come from very far away. In the early 1800s, there was no way to ship food long distances quickly enough to avoid spoilage.

Over time the country grew. Large cities sprang up, and many people came to these urban centers to work in factories. By the 1860s, most Americans no longer grew their own food and there were far fewer family farms. As a result, Americans lost direct control over their food supply.

An expanding railway system along with the invention of refrigerated railroad cars allowed a sizable food industry to take root in the United States. Americans depended on large businesses for what they ate, and the food on their tables sometimes came from hundreds of miles away. Often many people were involved in getting the U.S. food supply from suppliers to households. Usually there were distributors or middlemen in addition to the farmers and ranchers who actually grew the food or raised the cattle. Yet there was no one in charge of regulating or overseeing this vast process. Consumers couldn't always be sure that the food they bought was wholesome and safe.

Workers pack grapes from California into a refrigerator car for transport to the East Coast in the 1920s. Refrigeration allowed fresh produce to be sold far from the fields where it was grown.

By the early-1900s, meat processing had become a year-round business. Enormous numbers of livestock were slaughtered and shipped to various parts of the country. Filthy conditions existed in most meatpacking houses, and too often diseased livestock found their way into the food supply.

The United States was a country of meat eaters, so this posed a serious public health risk. At first, individual states took measures to protect consumers. But before long, some states resented the regulations passed by others. Still other states offered no protection whatsoever to consumers.

TAINTED MILK

The meat industry was not the only place where American consumers were at risk. There was also a problem with drinking raw or unpasteurized milk. The French scientist Louis Pasteur had come up with the process of pasteurization in the 1850s. The process

www.usatoday.com

USA TODAY

Life
SECTION D

August 7, 2006

From the Pages of USA TODAY

Raw milk: Fit for human consumption?

Proponents say it's good for you; health officials say it's dangerous

John Langlois feels so strongly about the benefits of unpasteurized goat milk that he pays $19 a gallon [3.8 liters] to have it shipped from a South Carolina dairy to his home in Estillfork, Ala. He credits it with giving him more energy, curing his grandson's chronic diarrhea when he was an infant and keeping the boy "steady" rather than "bouncing off the walls" now that he's 5.

Elizabeth Benner of Rochester, N.Y., drives 45 minutes each way to a dairy to get a week's worth of raw cow's milk for nine families in the milk club she organized.

She says she was "really struggling" on a low-fat, vegan [no animal products] diet but regained her strength when she added whole raw milk and cream to her diet.

Christina Trecaso of Copley, Ohio, is in a herd share program. She and 150 other families pay boarding costs for "their" cows and take their profits in milk, butter and cream. For her, it's about "buying food that is minimally processed, food that is procured in a 100-mile [161-kilometer] radius.... It's about relationships and shaking the hand that feeds you."

Each of them is a strong believer in the

allows milk to have a longer shelf life (to last longer before spoiling). Yet in the early 1900s, unpasteurized milk was still sold and at times with devastating consequences.

Scientists found that the bacteria in contaminated milk were often connected to typhoid, scarlet fever, and cholera epidemics. A 1903 study on infant deaths in New York City showed a strong connection between the 10 percent infant mortality rate there and unpasteurized milk.

Still another study at about the same time revealed that more than 8 percent of the milk supply in Boston, Massachusetts, was importance of unpasteurized milk. Each of them is also breaking the law. Selling raw milk is illegal in 25 states and the District of Columbia. In New York, dairies providing raw must be state certified. Benner's is not.

But each believes that the benefits outweigh the expense, inconvenience and illegality. They've got lots of company.

Advocates of raw milk are behind legislative efforts in Tennessee, Ohio, Kentucky and Nebraska to legalize selling raw milk. Moves to introduce legislation have begun in North Carolina and Maryland.

But this is a dangerous game, public health officials say.

- In June, more than 58 people in Wisconsin became ill with *Campylobacter jejuni* from unpasteurized cheese curds.
- In January, five people became ill with campylobacteriosis after drinking raw milk from a dairy in Larimer County, Colo.
- In December 2005, six children in

Washington state were infected with a potentially deadly form of *E. coli* O157:H7 bacteria from drinking unpasteurized milk.

No matter how clean the cows or the barn, all milk contains fecal material, says William Keene, senior epidemiologist in Oregon's Acute and Communicable Disease Program. "This is what happens when you hose down a cow and then put a vacuum down at the south end of it."

For those who are convinced that pasteurized milk is unhealthy, there's little that health workers can do to change their minds, says Michael Lynch, a foodborne-illness expert at the Centers for Disease Control and Prevention.

"But we want to get the word out to people who may not understand," he says. "If you explained the dangers to them, they would probably not want to drink the raw milk. They're confusing it with organic, and organic has positive connotations."

—Elizabeth Weise

contaminated by bovine (cattle) tuberculosis. The symptoms of this disease, which largely affected children, included high fevers, painful stomach cramps, and weight loss. When the disease infected the spine, the ill person's bones might become deformed. Pasteurization could prevent the disease from spreading to humans through milk.

While some people wanted a law to ensure that milk be pasteurized, not everyone favored the idea. Some dairy farmers claimed that their profits would suffer. Milk distributors were threatening to pay them less for their product, since the cost of maintaining large pasteurizing facilities was likely to be high.

Meanwhile, public health experts and reformers stressed that government regulation was essential if disease was to be prevented. They couldn't afford to leave these decisions up to business owners. A broader national approach to food safety was needed.

THE DEPARTMENT OF AGRICULTURE TO THE RESCUE

Many of the country's elected leaders agreed. As early as 1862, President Abraham Lincoln felt that the federal government should take a role in regulating food safety and distribution. The president established the U.S. Department of Agriculture (USDA) and hired a chemist named Charles M. Wetherill to spearhead the effort to regulate food safety. Wetherill was asked to lead a USDA agency known as the Bureau of Chemistry. This was the forerunner of the Food and Drug Administration (FDA).

Both the FDA and the USDA have the task of safeguarding the U.S. food supply. The USDA inspects and regulates meat and poultry products to ensure that they are safe, wholesome, and accurately labeled. The FDA inspects and regulates most other foods Americans eat. The goal of both agencies is to prevent problems before they start. To do so, thousands of chemists, microbiologists, physicians, veterinarians, pharmacologists, lawyers, and other staff members work together to identify risks and vulnerable areas within our food supply.

PROBLEMS

On the whole, these agencies do a good job. Yet at times, some lapses have seriously affected the U.S. food supply. In 1993 an outbreak of *E. coli* O157:H7 swept through the Pacific Northwest. The outbreak resulted in four hundred illnesses and four deaths. In 2002 27 million pounds [12 million kg] of poultry contaminated with *Listeria*

USDA scientists inspect a carcass. The USDA and FDA are responsible for safeguarding the U.S. food supply.

bacteria were recalled. Nine deaths and more than fifty illnesses in the Northeast were believed to have stemmed from that case. Other incidents have occurred as well.

As President Barack Obama noted on March 14, 2009, in his weekly address to the American people:

In recent years, we've seen a number of problems with the food making its way to our kitchen tables. In 2006, it was contaminated spinach. In 2008, it was *Salmonella* in peppers and possibly tomatoes. And just this year [2009], bad peanut products led to hundreds of illnesses and cost nine people their lives—a painful reminder of how tragic the consequences can be when food producers act irresponsibly and government is unable to do its job. . . . When I heard peanut products were

www.usatoday.com

Money
SECTION B

March 2, 2007

From the Pages of USA TODAY

Kraft expands chicken recall
Issued after Listeria found in package

A chicken-product recall has grown to 2.8 million pounds [1.3 million kg], making it one of the largest meat or poultry recalls since 2004.

The initial recall of 52,650 pounds [23,882 kg] of Oscar Mayer/Louis Rich Chicken Breast Strips—Grilled was announced Feb. 18 after *Listeria* bacteria was found in one package.

As a precaution, Kraft Foods, the product's owner, expanded the recall to all its products made at the same plant. It did more tests and found more *Listeria*, says Kraft's Elisabeth Wenner. *Listeria* can cause serious infections in some people.

The recall now covers Oscar Mayer/Louis Rich Chicken Breast Strips and Cuts in 6-ounce [170 grams] and 12-ounce [340 g] packages with a "use by" date of May 28, 2007, or earlier. The packaging bears the number "P-19676" inside the Department of Agriculture mark of inspection. Initially, the recall affected products best used by April 19, 2007.

No illnesses have been reported. The products, distributed to retailers nationwide, were made by Carolina Culinary Foods, a manufacturer for Kraft. The plant is not producing pending an investigation, USDA spokesman Steven Cohen says. The USDA Wednesday announced the expanded recall. "We run a safe plant—and we'll do whatever it takes to keep it safe," Carolina Culinary said in a statement.

Food recalls may grow as investigations widen, says Neal Hooker, an associate professor of economics at Ohio State University who has studied meat and poultry recalls. Contamination may occur if products aren't properly cooked or bacteria in the environment gets into a package before it is sealed, he says.

—*Julie Schmit*

being contaminated earlier this year, I immediately thought of my seven-year-old daughter, Sasha, who has peanut butter sandwiches for lunch probably three times a week. No parent should have to worry that their child is going to get sick from their lunch.... Worse, these incidents reflect a troubling trend that's seen the average number of outbreaks from contaminated produce and other foods grow to nearly 350 a year—up from 100 a year in the early 1990s.

Part of the problem has to do with outdated laws and regulations still governing food safety in the United States. Some of these laws were written as early as 1906, when President Theodore Roosevelt was in office. They haven't been updated since. The need for a new approach is crucial since much of the American food supply comes from international sources.

In 2006 the FDA processed fifteen million shipments of food arriving in the United States from other nations. That number shows a 60 percent rise in edible imports from 2003. The FDA has to oversee the safety of food products from over 230 countries and more than three hundred thousand manufacturers. In many of these nations,

This refrigerated warehouse in California stores imported food that the FDA has tagged for further inspection.

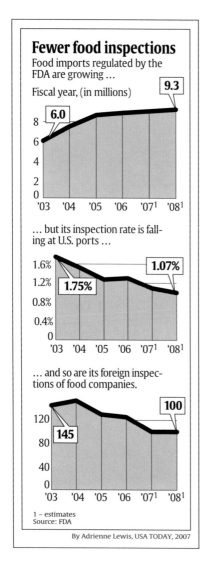

Fewer food inspections

Food imports regulated by the FDA are growing ...

Fiscal year, (in millions)

6.0 **9.3**

8
6
4
2
0

'03 '04 '05 '06 '07[1] '08[1]

... but its inspection rate is falling at U.S. ports ...

1.6%
1.2% **1.75%**
0.8%
0.4%
0 **1.07%**

'03 '04 '05 '06 '07[1] '08[1]

... and so are its foreign inspections of food companies.

120
80 **145**
40
0 **100**

'03 '04 '05 '06 '07[1] '08[1]

1 – estimates
Source: FDA

By Adrienne Lewis, USA TODAY, 2007

controls on food safety tend to be weaker than in the United States.

To make matters worse, the FDA has been understaffed and poorly funded in recent years. It had been able to inspect only 7,000 of 150,000 food processing plants and warehouses each year. That leaves about 95 percent of them uninspected.

SOLUTIONS

In response, President Obama has taken steps to change things. He created a Food Safety Working Group to look into upgrading food safety laws and to enhance coordination between the different government agencies involved. The Department of Agriculture is taking action as well. It's closing a loophole in the system to ensure that diseased cattle stay out of the U.S. food supply.

Ideally under current regulations, cows that can't stand or walk on their own must be rejected, as they may be diseased. Yet a dangerous exception to this rule permits a cow that has passed an initial inspection to get through even if it cannot stand or walk afterward. Such animals can be slaughtered for food if a second inspection determines that they are not ill but have an injury such as a broken leg.

KEEPING OUR FOOD SAFE | 93

Timeline of U.S. Food Safety Regulations

- 1862: President Abraham Lincoln forms the U.S. Department of Agriculture.

- 1870s: Expanding railroads and refrigerator cars allow the development of a large meat packing industry. Individual states attempt regulation to control livestock diseases, but such measures are mostly ineffective.

- 1906: President Theodore Roosevelt responds to a public outcry for federal inspectors to be placed in meat packing houses. The Federal Meat Inspection Act is passed.

- 1931: The Food and Drug Administration is formally established.

- 1957: After World War II (1939–1945) the poultry industry grows tremendously. Congress passes the Poultry Products Inspection Act to ensure that the poultry and poultry products sold are wholesome and safe.

- 1967–1968: The Federal Meat Inspection Act is amended to become the Wholesome Meat Act of 1967. The following year, the Poultry Products Inspection Act is amended to become the Poultry Products Inspection Act of 1968. Meat- and poultry-inspecting programs merge into a single program.

- 2009: The USDA permanently bans the slaughter of cows too sick or weak to stand on their own. President Barack Obama announces the creation of the Food Safety Working Group to take steps toward revamping the nation's public health regulations.

www.usatoday.com

USA TODAY
Life
SECTION D

July 8, 2009

From the Pages of USA TODAY

FDA: Improved food safety measures, communication ahead

Priority is to prevent initial contamination

It's tough enough these days just finding enough money to put food on the table, and Americans shouldn't also have to worry about whether it's safe to eat, Vice President Biden said today as he announced proposals to make the U.S. food supply more safe.

Biden and Health and Human Services Secretary Kathleen Sebelius announced recommendations from President Obama's Food Safety Working Group,

a panel of administration officials and outside experts created in March. Biden and Sebelius are co-chairs of the group.

"The focus is to have a completely different emphasis than we've had in the past," Biden said. "We're going to make our new priority preventing (contamination) from happening in the first place."

Coming changes, which can be enacted without Congressional approval:

• Within 90 days, an improved

Under a new rule proposed by the USDA, this exception will no longer be allowed, as it leaves too much room for error and abuse. The newly proposed change followed the release of a secretly recorded videotape that showed California meat plant workers using forklifts and electric prods on animals unable to stand in an effort to get them to the slaughterhouse.

"There should be no longer even a slim possibility of transporting a cow to market that is too weak to rise or walk on its own," U.S. Department of Agriculture secretary Ed Schafer told reporters. "This action sends a clear message to consumers in both domestic and international markets that we will continue to uphold the highest individual alert system at www. foodsafety.gov to give consumers immediate access to "critical food-safety information" such as recalls.

- New safeguards designed to cut *Salmonella* in raw eggs, *E. coli* in ground beef and other pathogens in leafy greens, melons and tomatoes.
- A better tracking system to pinpoint the origins of outbreaks.
- Better communications between agencies that regulate food safety.
- New positions at the Food and Drug Administration and the U.S. Department of Agriculture to oversee food safety.

George Washington University [Washington, D.C.] food-safety expert Michael Taylor began work Monday as senior adviser to FDA commissioner Margaret Hamburg. He calls the recommendations "a huge undertaking.

It's a transformative strategy."

The new proposals give the FDA "real teeth" in requiring companies to track food-safety problems and make that information available to the government, Taylor says. It will require public-health-oriented performance standards and risk-based inspection programs.

For example, in this summer's recall of Nestle Toll House Brand refrigerated cookie dough, it was revealed that when FDA inspectors toured the plant, the company—well within its rights under current rules—refused to provide inspectors with complaint logs, pest-control records and other information. Under the new rules, the company would be required to do so, Taylor says.

The switch won't be easy. "It's going to take all hands on deck at FDA to figure out how to do this right," he says.

—*Elizabeth Weise*

standards to protect our food supply and deliver the highest quality products." Schafer further noted that "by reducing the incentive to send weak and marginal cattle to slaughter, it will [also] reduce the likelihood that those animals will be subjected to inhumane handling at processing plants."

In addition to these measures, the government will also be increasing the number of food inspectors and modernizing food safety labs with a billion-dollar investment. As the future approaches, Americans can feel more confident than ever as they sit down each night at the dinner table.

FOOD SAFETY AT HOME

The United States has one of the safest food supply systems in the world. Strict guidelines at many levels keep it that way. Yet for food to remain safe from the time it leaves the store until it reaches the dinner table, people should be aware of some important precautions they should take. Many people think that they will know if food has gone bad by the way it looks and smells, but this is not always true. Everyone should be aware of how to best pick, prepare, and preserve the foods we eat.

FOOD SHOPPING

Armed with the right information, anyone can become a smart shopper. It starts with knowing when to do your food shopping. If on a particular day, you find that you have other errands to do in addition to shopping for food, go food shopping last. That way, frozen items and foods that should be refrigerated will not be exposed to warm temperatures for very long. Some people keep a cooler in their car for these items. If that isn't possible, skip extra stops on the way home and put perishable items away as soon as you can.

Smart shoppers practice other tips while selecting the foods they purchase. This includes paying close attention to products that have dates stamped on them. Usually these are perishable items such as meat, poultry, eggs, and dairy products. Sometimes products are stamped with a "sell-by" date. This date lets the store know how long to display the product for sale. Check these dates when shopping, and purchase these items before the sell-by date.

Other types of dates may be on products too. These may include a "best if used by (or before)" date. This date does not mean that the product is not safe to use after that date. It simply advises the shopper to use it by that date for the best quality or flavor. Still other packaging may have a "use by" date. The manufacturer determines this date, and it is the last day suggested for use of the product at its peak quality. These are really just two ways of indicating the same thing.

It's a good idea to eat these products before any of these dates expire. However, if a date should expire while the

Nutrition Facts
Serving Size 2 tbsp (30g)
Servings Per Container About 15

Amount Per Serving

Calories 60   Calories from Fat 45

"Sell-by" dates are often stamped on dairy products, such as this sour cream container.

product is in your refrigerator, it probably is still fine for a short time afterward, if it has been properly handled and refrigerated. If a perishable item has been frozen, the expiration date is no longer relevant. Food items that are frozen continuously remain safe for longer periods of time.

The federal government only requires that infant formula and some baby food have product dates. More than twenty states require that a number of additional foods be dated too. But in some states, almost no foods have dates on them.

Therefore, it is up to the shopper to look carefully at the food before buying it. Refrigerated items taken from a refrigerator case should feel cold to the touch. The frozen foods you buy should be frozen solid. Put milk and other refrigerated and frozen items in your cart last so they are out of the refrigerator or the freezer for the least time possible.

Pass up canned products with dented, cracked, or bulging containers. Fruits and vegetables should appear fresh, and meat should be firm to the touch and not have a greenish tint to it. If you are buying eggs, open the carton to check if any are cracked or broken. Don't buy cracked or broken eggs. Be sure to check the expiration date on egg cartons as well. That is the last date that the store can sell those eggs as fresh. Some egg cartons have a federal grade mark on them, such as Grade AA. That means the expiration date cannot be any longer than thirty days after the eggs were packed into the carton. Eggs purchased before the expiration date can be safely used for three to five weeks from the day they were bought.

Sometimes, raw poultry, meat, and seafood drip. These juices may contain bacteria. It is important that these foods and their juices are kept away from other foods so as not to contaminate them. Raw poultry, meat, and seafood should be placed in separate plastic bags before being bagged with other foods at the checkout counter.

Carefully check all fresh fruits and vegetables before purchasing them. Pass up any that are bruised or damaged. Harmful bacteria can enter through these openings. Only buy cut-up fruits and vegetables if they are properly refrigerated or surrounded by ice.

STORING FOOD

Put away all refrigerated and frozen items as soon as you get home from shopping. Keeping these foods cold is crucial to stopping bacteria from rapidly multiplying or producing harmful toxins. For this reason, the refrigerator should be set at 40°F (4°C) with the freezer unit at 0°F (−17°C). If you suspect that your refrigerator is not cold enough, you can check it with an appliance thermometer. These are fairly inexpensive and can be purchased at most hardware stores. As a rule, a refrigerator should be kept as cold as possible without freezing the milk and lettuce. Don't overpack your refrigerator with food. The cool air needs to be able to circulate to keep food at the proper temperature and safe to eat.

Any cut-up fruits and vegetables should be immediately refrigerated. If you later cut or peel fruit or vegetables yourself, these pieces should also be refrigerated within two hours of being cut.

Fresh Produce—How to Store It

Some fruits and vegetables should be refrigerated. Others should be kept at room temperature. This guide will help you know how to best store different types of produce.

Keep these items refrigerated. They will spoil sooner at room temperature:

- Apples, artichokes, asparagus, beans, beets, blueberries, broccoli, brussels sprouts, cabbage, Belgian endive, carrots, cauliflower, celery, cherries, sweet corn, cranberries, cucumbers, eggplant, gingerroot, grapes, fresh herbs, leeks, lettuce and other greens, mushrooms, green onions, parsnips, peas, peppers, pineapple, new potatoes, radishes, raspberries, rhubarb, strawberries, squash, citrus fruits, and turnips.

Keep these fruits at room temperature until they ripen. Once they are ripe, refrigerate them until you are ready to eat them:

- Apricots, avocados, kiwis, mangoes, melons, nectarines, papaya, peaches, pears, plums, and tomatoes.

Keep these items at room temperature rather than in the refrigerator:

- Bananas, garlic, globe onions, pumpkins, and rutabagas.

Eggs are another food that need to be refrigerated. Keep them in their carton so you can check the expiration date on it.

If you do not plan to use raw meat, poultry, or seafood right away, it is best to freeze these items. Be sure to place the raw meat, poultry, and seafood you plan to cook soon on a plate in the refrigerator so that their juices don't drip onto other food. This will stop any harmful bacteria in the juice from contaminating the food.

Some people store these products on the bottom shelf of the refrigerator, where they can't drip on food below. Another safety

Refrigerating Uncooked Meat and Other Products

How long can you safely keep uncooked meats, poultry, and eggs in the refrigerator before cooking them? Just check the guide below:

- Poultry: refrigerator storage time — 1 or 2 days

- Beef, veal, pork, and lamb: refrigerator storage time — 3 to 5 days

- Ground meat and ground poultry: refrigerator storage time — 1 to 2 days

- Fresh variety meats (liver, tongue, brain, kidneys): refrigerator storage time — 1 to 2 days

- Cured ham: refrigerator storage time — 5 to 7 days

- Sausage from pork, beef, or turkey: refrigerator storage time — 1 to 2 days

- Eggs: refrigerator storage time — 3 to 5 weeks

June 17, 2009

From the Pages of USA TODAY

As new chief takes over, 'FDA has a lot on its plate'

Hamburg will tackle agency's expanding roles

Margaret Hamburg figured she'd follow her parents' example and pursue a career in academic medicine, perhaps as an endocrinologist [a doctor trained to treat disorders of the endocrine system].

"I'd never planned a career as a public health official," said Hamburg, who was recently confirmed as the second woman to helm the Food and Drug Administration.

But she changed her mind when, as an internal medicine resident in New York in the early 1980s, she began caring for patients with the condition that would come to be called AIDS. She wanted to understand how to translate medical discoveries into patient care.

A quarter-century later, Hamburg, 53, leads the federal agency that arguably has the biggest impact on the public's health.

As she and Joshua Sharfstein, principal deputy commissioner at the FDA, noted last week in *The New England Journal of Medicine*, the agency oversees more than $2 trillion in medical products, food and other consumer goods. And just last week, Congress overwhelmingly voted to add tobacco products to the list. As Hamburg says, "the FDA has a lot on its plate already."

Adding to the agency's workload is the fact that many of the products it regulates are manufactured in other countries. "It represents a tremendous challenge," Hamburg says, adding that the FDA must step up as a leader on the global scene.

—*Rita Rubin*

measure is to cover all refrigerated foods with foil or plastic wrap to protect them from contamination.

Keep canned items on a shelf in a cool, dry place. Never place any canned goods above a stove, under a sink, or in a damp garage or basement. Avoid exposing canned products to either very high or very low temperatures.

PREPARING FOOD

Always thoroughly wash your hands for at least twenty seconds with warm soapy water before working with food. Dry your hands well, since wet hands can more easily spread bacteria. Take measures to keep harmful bacteria out of your food preparation area as well. Kitchen towels and other cloths used to wipe counter areas can easily harbor germs. Wash these items frequently in hot soapy water. Start off each day with a clean, dry wiping cloth. Sponges are especially difficult to clean and can harbor bacteria in their nooks and crannies.

Meat, poultry, and seafood spoil quickly. So it is especially important to keep these foods away from other items when preparing a meal. If you cut meat, poultry, or seafood on a cutting board, wash your hands, the cutting board, and the knife you used, before using that same cutting board and knife again. To thoroughly sanitize a cutting board, use a solution of one-half teaspoon [2.5 milliliters] of liquid chlorine bleach to 1 quart [1 liter] of water. Thoroughly rinse the board before using it again.

Also thoroughly wash a platter that held raw food before using it to serve cooked foods. It is crucial to keep raw meat, poultry, and

Proper hand washing requires thoroughly rinsing hands with running water after lathering with soap for twenty to thirty seconds.

seafood away from ready-to-eat foods such as salads, fruits, and bread. These foods will not be cooked before they are eaten, so any bacteria transferred to them will not be killed.

Thaw frozen items either in the refrigerator or in a microwave oven. Use the defrost setting to thaw food in a microwave, and be sure to cook the food immediately afterward. Slowly thawing meat, poultry, and seafood on a kitchen counter is like sending out an invitation to harmful bacteria. Bacteria will frequently begin to grow in the outer layers of the food while the inside of the item is still frozen.

The same is true when marinating meat, poultry, or seafood. For marinating, the food is placed in a marinade—a bowl of sauce or another mixture—to soak in the flavor. Depending on the recipe, the meat, poultry, or seafood may have to remain in the marinade for several hours or longer. To make sure the food remains free of harmful bacteria, it should marinate in the refrigerator.

Take care preparing fruits and vegetables. Wash the produce under cold running water. Do not use soap or detergent on these items, but thoroughly scrub all fruits and vegetables that have hard outer surfaces with a clean produce brush. These would include melons, citrus fruits, tomatoes, carrots, kiwis, potatoes, and grapefruits.

The skins of vegetables and fruits that grow on the ground or under it can become contaminated by bacteria from the soil or by contact with wildlife. Cantaloupes need to be washed especially well since their skin is rough and netted. Sometimes bacteria can become trapped in the netting.

An improperly washed fruit or vegetable can become contaminated when cut. Cutting brings dust and bacteria from the outside to the interior. Be sure to cut away any damaged or bruised spots on fruits and vegetables. Harmful bacteria can thrive in these areas. Remember to clean your knife well after cutting out the bruised and damaged parts.

COOKING FOOD

The heat used to cook food also kills harmful bacteria. It is important to cook foods at the right temperature and crucial to thoroughly cook all meat, poultry, and seafood. Use a meat thermometer to be sure that your food is properly cooked both inside and outside. Meat, poultry, and seafood should never be cooked in an oven set below 325°F (162°C). When these foods are properly cooked, the juices flowing from them should be clear.

Do not partially cook meat, poultry, seafood, or casseroles containing these items one day and finish cooking them the next. Partially cooked foods offer an excellent opportunity for bacteria to grow. Fully cook all your meat, poultry, and seafood to destroy any harmful bacteria that might be present. Once these items are completely cooked, they can be quickly cooled and then reheated later.

A lot of attention has been paid to cooking meat, but it is also important to cook eggs correctly. The bacteria *Salmonella* can grow inside a fresh egg even before its shell has been broken. An egg should be cooked until both the yolk and the white portion are firm. No part of the egg should be runny. If you like scrambled eggs, be sure to scramble them until they are dry.

USA TODAY Snapshots®

Is it done yet?

Twenty-two percent of people say they use a meat thermometer when barbecuing. Recommended temperatures to reduce the chance of illness:

Hamburgers, sausages, pork chops, steaks to medium-well
160°

165° Hot dogs, chicken or turkey burgers

170° Poultry breasts

180° Poultry thighs, wings, drumsticks or whole bird

Source: Impulse Research Corp. for American Dietetic Association and ConAgra Foods Foundation

By Rebecca F. Johnson and Sam Ward, USA TODAY, 2004

Cooking Times Vary

Here's a handy guide for cooking meat.

Using a meat thermometer to check the internal temperature of cooked meat can help avoid foodborne diseases.

- Cook beef, veal, and lamb steaks and roasts to 160°F (71°C) for medium and to 170°F (77°C) for well done.

- Cook ground pork and beef to 160°F (71°C).

- Cook poultry breasts to 170°F (77°C).

- Cook a whole chicken or turkey to 180°F (82°C). Test for the right temperature by placing the meat thermometer in the bird's thigh. Stuffing inside the bird should be cooked to 165°F (74°C).

- Cook a fish to 145°F (63°C), or until the flesh is opaque and separates easily with a fork. Though some restaurants serve sushi (raw fish) as well as very rare fish, you take a chance in ordering these items. Fish that is not thoroughly cooked can contain bacteria and parasites.

- Cook shrimp, lobsters, and crabs until the meat looks pearly and opaque.

- Cook clams, oysters, and mussels until their shells open.

Do not leave either raw or cooked eggs out of the refrigerator for more than two hours. Remember: 40 to 140°F (4 to 60°C) is the danger zone for food spoilage. Food is most likely to spoil within that temperature range and the average room temperature is about 70°F (21°C). In recipes that call for raw or partially cooked eggs, such as some homemade ice creams, mousses, salad dressings, and eggnog, use pasteurized eggs or an egg substitute.

MICROWAVE COOKING

Microwave ovens are terrific time-savers, and in some families, much of the food is cooked in a microwave. Food can be cooked safely in a microwave oven if you remember that microwaves cook food differently from conventional ovens. Special precautions have to be followed to cook food safely.

Microwaving meals can leave cold spots in food where bacteria can multiply. So it's a good idea to microwave food in containers that have lids. The steam generated within the container helps to cook the food more thoroughly. Another choice is to cover the cooking dish with plastic wrap. Make sure that the plastic wrap only touches the dish—not the food in it. Puncture the plastic wrap with a fork to allow some steam to escape during cooking. Stirring and rotating the food helps it to cook more evenly in a microwave. This is especially important if the microwave oven doesn't have a turntable.

Often microwave recipes or packages direct you to let the food stand for some minutes after it is removed from the microwave oven. It is important to follow these directions since the food is actually still cooking during this time. To be completely sure that the food has thoroughly cooked, use a meat thermometer. Check the food in several places to determine that it is evenly cooked throughout.

www.usatoday.com

USA TODAY

Life
SECTION D

October 15, 2008

From the Pages of USA TODAY

New warning over microwaving raw frozen chicken entrees

Misreading label can result in Salmonella

The U.S. Department of Agriculture once again is warning consumers to read the label when cooking frozen chicken entrees amid the fourth *Salmonella* outbreak in three years linked to raw frozen entrees.

There have been 34 cases this year of *Salmonella* food poisoning in at least 12 states from eating undercooked chicken.

In each case, consumers thought breaded or pre-browned frozen chicken entrees were cooked, but they were raw.

In March, the USDA issued a public health alert to remind consumers that the "instructions on the package need to be followed for safety," spokeswoman Laura Reiser says.

The agency didn't name a particular manufacturer but did say the entrees were sold as chicken Kiev, chicken cordon bleu or stuffed chicken breasts.

The products were not meant to be microwaved, they didn't include microwave instructions, and the labels said the chicken was raw.

But because the entrees were breaded or pre-browned, some consumers thought they also were precooked and simply warmed them in the microwave. Microwaving did not get them hot enough to kill *Salmonella* bacteria in the raw chicken.

Food manufacturers have modified labels on such chicken products several times over the past year. Older labels used phrases such as "ready to cook" or "not precooked."

But Kirk Smith, head of the foodborne disease unit of the Minnesota Department of Health, says people are microwaving the products without focusing on the label stating the entree is raw, and despite the lack of microwave instructions.

"We wish the labels would be even more emphatic," he says.

Minnesota health officials met with producers of chicken products and were told that precooking wasn't an option because it has an effect on the texture and appearance of the chicken.

He says the best solution would be "electronic pasteurization," also known as irradiation, which would kill the *Salmonella* but leave the chicken raw.

—Elizabeth Weise

DEALING WITH LEFTOVERS

All leftovers should be promptly refrigerated, ideally within one to two hours. A large amount of leftover food will cool more quickly if you divide it and store it in individual shallow containers. Spread out the containers in the refrigerator so that the cool air can circulate and quickly chill the food. Be sure to spread out thick foods such as sauces and stews in the container so that all parts of it can cool speedily. It is also a good idea to cut large chunks of meat into smaller pieces.

Leftovers do not safely last for very long. They should be eaten within the next two days. If the leftovers are going to be packed to go, they should be put in insulated carriers or lunch boxes with a cold pack. Whether taken to school or work, these lunches should never be left in direct sunlight or on a warm radiator. If you are going to reheat the leftovers to eat at home, make certain that the food is piping hot before eating it. Lukewarm leftovers might not be safe to eat. Remember if you heat leftovers more than once, recontamination is possible at each recooling and reheating. Be sure to cook them thoroughly.

WHAT ABOUT THE WATER?

Many people drink bottled water. Some do this because they believe that their tap water is unhealthy. Certainly, the advertisements for bottled water make it seem like a cleaner, safer, and healthier alternative.

Scientific tests on both bottled water and tap water revealed that the only difference between the two is price. In some cases, bottled water can cost up to one thousand times more than tap water. Tap water is just as safe as bottled water. That may be partly because both tap and bottled water are required to meet government-regulated standards for purity.

A study by University of Geneva (Switzerland) researcher Catherine Ferrier showed that the only difference between tap water and some bottled waters is that one comes in a bottle and the other comes through a pipe. When you look beyond the bottled water commercials and read the labels on bottled water, you'll see that the water often does not come from an exotic place, such as the one pictured on the label. If the label or the cap reads "from a municipal source" or "from a community water system," then you are actually buying bottled tap water. About one-quarter of the bottled water sold is simply tap water in a bottle. Glacier Clear Water is not from a glacier in Alaska or somewhere in Europe. It is tap water from Greeneville, Tennessee.

If you still wish to purchase bottled water, always look at the bottles carefully before you buy them. Make certain that the seal on the bottle hasn't been broken and that there is no debris in the water. Do not reuse the old bottles unless they have been thoroughly cleaned and sanitized.

IN CASE OF EMERGENCY!

Refrigeration is a large factor in keeping the foods we eat safe. But what if there's a loss of power due to a hurricane, fire, high winds, snow, flooding, or ice? It is best to keep a supply of easily stored food on hand for these emergencies. These items can include dried fruits, canned fruits and vegetables, jars of peanut butter and jelly, small packages of cereal, granola bars, crackers, nonfat dry milk, and small juice boxes. Keep a manually operated can opener as well. An electric can opener won't work without power. You should also have a three-day supply of commercially bottled water. That means at least 1 gallon [4 liters] a day for each person in your household.

The following measures, suggested by the U.S. Department of Agriculture's Food Safety and Inspection Service, will prove helpful during a power outage:

- Keep the refrigerator and freezer doors closed as much as possible to maintain the cold temperature. The refrigerator will keep food safely cold for about four hours if it is unopened. A full freezer will hold the temperature for approximately forty-eight hours (twenty-four hours if it is only half full even if the freezer door remains closed).
- Discard refrigerated perishable foods such as meat, poultry, fish, soft cheeses, and deli items after four hours without power.
- Store food on shelves that will be safely away from contaminated water in case of flooding.
- Do not eat any food that may have come in contact with floodwater.
- Discard any food that is not in a waterproof container if there is any chance that it has come in contact with floodwater. Food containers that are not waterproof include those with screw caps, snap lids, pull tops, and crimped caps. Also, discard cardboard juice/milk/baby formula boxes and home-canned food if they have come in contact with floodwater. These items cannot be effectively cleaned and sanitized.
- Drink only bottled water if flooding has occurred.
- Never taste a food to determine its safety.
- When in doubt, throw it out!

REPORTING FOODBORNE ILLNESS

Suspected cases of foodborne disease should be reported to the health department in your area. Local health departments are an important link in the nationwide system of keeping the food supply

June 29, 2009

From the Pages of USA TODAY

Food cost vs. safety

It's tempting not to waste, but when in doubt, toss it

Times are tough and food is expensive. So a lot of us are standing in front of refrigerators or pantries these days asking: Should I toss it or eat it?

"I'm hearing these questions every day," says Maribel Alonso, a food safety specialist at the U.S. Department of Agriculture's Meat and Poultry Hotline. "People are more concerned now about throwing away food."

Of course, most people understand why they shouldn't eat potato salad that has been left in the sun for six hours. That's a well-known recipe for food poisoning. But some remain shockingly unsure of certain threats. Alonso says she has been asked if it's safe to eat roasted turkey kept in the refrigerator for three months. (No: The safe storage time on that turkey is a mere four days.)

Susan Reef, president of US Food Safety Corp., which runs a commercial website (usfoodsafety.com), says one frugal reader asked if it would be OK to finish the gourmet coffee drink left on her desk overnight. (No: There's nothing bacteria like better than warm liquid, plus time.) And she has heard that college-kid classic: Will it really hurt me to eat the pizza left out in the box overnight? (Yes, it might: After two hours, it should go in the fridge or in the trash.)

Other questions, though, are tougher, and experts don't always agree. For example, Alonso says that if she brings home a broken egg, she discards it. Doug Powell, a food safety expert at Kansas State University, puts it straight into a batch of pancake batter, cooks it thoroughly and serves it.

"It's just messy, but if it's been kept cold, it should be OK," he says.

USDA guidelines on food safety are conservative, Alonso says. The philosophy: "When in doubt, throw it out."

—Kim Painter

safe. According to the Centers for Disease Control and Prevention, calls from concerned citizens are often how outbreaks are first detected. The system works best when everyone participates.

CHAPTER NINE

OUT AND ABOUT— EATING AWAY FROM HOME

L ife in modern times can be very busy. Nearly everyone has things to do and places to go. As a result, people do not always eat at home. That makes it important to learn how to safely enjoy all kinds of foods when you are away from home.

DINING OUT

When dining out, make smart choices about where to eat as well as what to order. Do not eat at a restaurant that looks dirty. No bins overflowing with garbage should be outside it, as this could attract rats. The silverware, linens, glasses, and floor should all be clean. The servers should also look neat and clean and not have any open sores on their faces or hands. The restrooms should be clean as well. If these public areas aren't clean, then it is unlikely that the kitchen will be very clean either.

Restaurants are inspected by the local board of health to see that they meet sanitation regulations and have adequate kitchen facilities. Diners can find out how a particular restaurant scored on its most recent inspection. In some areas, restaurants are required to post their most recent inspection score where the public can see it.

When dining out, you can protect yourself from foodborne illnesses in other ways as well. When placing your order, be specific about how you'd like your food cooked. When you order a hamburger, ask that it be well done. If it is still pink inside when it is served, don't hesitate to send it back.

If you are unable to finish your meal at a restaurant, it is fine to take the remainder with you. Just remember to refrigerate it as

A Nebraska State health inspector examines a restaurant kitchen.

soon as you get home. You may be taking home a piece of meat that has been on your plate all through dinner and dessert. Then it remained without refrigeration in the car during the ride home. It's wisest to eat what you brought home by the following day. If it needs to be reheated, be sure to heat it to 160°F (71°C) to kill any harmful bacteria.

STREET VENDORS

If you live in an urban area, you have probably seen vendors selling a variety of food products from their stainless steel carts. These merchants offer a broad range of food that often includes hot pretzels, hot dogs, hamburgers, chicken, pork, lamb, duck, and fish. Many city dwellers rely on them for a quick lunch or snack.

USA TODAY
HEALTH REPORTS:
DISEASES AND DISORDERS

April 16, 2009

From the Pages of USA TODAY

Domino's nightmare holds lessons for marketers

Companies have to learn how to handle social-media attacks

It's a PR nightmare scenario: A national fast-food chain has to respond to a video, spreading rapidly online, that shows one of its employees picking his nose and placing the result in the food he's making. That's exactly what Domino's, the nation's largest pizza delivery chain, has spent the past several days doing.

Two employees—fired and facing charges—posted a video on YouTube on Monday that shows one of them doing gross things to a Domino's sub sandwich he is making. Among them: sticking cheese pieces up his nose and passing gas on the salami.

The video had been viewed more than 550,000 times by Wednesday.

For Domino's, the PR response hasn't been easy. The video reflects some of the worst fears consumers have about food purchased from restaurants. The video and discussion of it has moved on to Facebook, Twitter and dozens of other social-networking sites.

But Domino's is getting fairly high marks from social-networking and crisis-management gurus about its response.

And marketers are getting an instant lesson in the dangers of an online world where just about anyone with a video camera and a grudge can bring a company to its knees with lightning speed.

"Nothing is local anymore," Domino's spokesman Tim McIntyre says. "That's the challenge of the Web world. Any two idiots with a video camera and a dumb idea can damage the reputation of a 50-year-old brand."

An arrest warrant was issued Wednesday for Michael Anthony Setzer, 32, of Conover, N.C., and Kristy Lynn Hammonds, 31, of Taylorsville, N.C., for food tampering, a felony in North Carolina, police say. McIntyre says Domino's is mulling a lawsuit.

As a result of the incident, Domino's is looking at banning video cameras in stores, McIntyre says.

—Bruce Horovitz

Be careful when buying from street vendors. Many start the day early with their carts filled with raw meat and poultry. Often the food remains unheated and unchilled for much of the day, providing a ripe breeding ground for disease-causing bacteria. Many street vendors seldom wash their hands throughout the day. Sometimes they even use the sinks in their carts to store food products. Street vendors have often been observed slicing meat with their bare hands, wiping their hands on a dirty rag, taking money from customers, and then going back to slicing meat. In addition, random tests of the food sold by street vendors in numerous cities revealed that the meat they sold was often undercooked.

These pushcart vendors are supposed to be licensed, but many operate illegally without permits. Yet even licensed street vendors frequently have at least one violation when they are inspected. These range from not having a working sink, so that they can wash their hands, to leaving meat out at a temperature warm enough for bacteria to grow. Other violations have included having dead roaches in their carts and storing raw beef directly on top of cooked beef. Even if you are very hungry, it is best not to buy food from street vendors. Find a better lunch or snack choice.

FOOD SAFETY WHILE CAMPING

The same food safety rules you rely on at home apply when you are camping. It is important to remember to keep hot foods hot and cold foods cold to prevent the growth of harmful bacteria. To keep food cold while you travel to a campsite, keep it in a cooler. Plastic, fiberglass, and steel coolers are available at camping supply stores for this purpose.

Cold food should be kept at 40°F (4°C) or below. To keep the items in your cooler at this temperature, you will need a cold source. Blocks of ice last longer than ice cubes, so some people fill clean, empty milk cartons with water and freeze them. These make excellent, inexpensive ice blocks. Frozen gel packs work well too. Fill the cooler with food that is already cold or frozen. Keep raw meat, poultry, and seafood tightly wrapped so their juices do not contaminate other foods in the cooler. While traveling to the campsite, always keep the cooler in the air-conditioned passenger section of the car—not in a hot trunk.

Even if you are going to use a campfire or bring a portable stove to the campsite, it's still probably safest to cook your food before you leave home. After it is cooked, quickly cool these items and transport them cold. You can reheat them after you've arrived.

Be Prepared!

Sometimes a little preparation goes a long way in camping. This is especially true when it comes to food. These days many campsites do not allow campfires or restrict them. Check to be sure that making a fire is permitted where you will be camping before packing and heading out without a portable stove. If you are permitted to build a fire, make sure that it is completely out before leaving the site. Burn any leftover food so that no garbage is left at the site.

If you are buying a portable stove, do not use it for the first time on your trip. Practice assembling it as well as lighting it before you leave home. Make sure that the stove is in good working order and that you have everything you need with you to cook with it.

When camping, it is best to carefully plan your meals and snacks in advance. Usually perishable foods can safely remain without refrigeration for two hours, but if it is very hot, the rules change. When the temperature rises above 90°F (32°C), perishable foods should not be left out for more than an hour. Keep these items in a cooler, surrounded by plenty of ice or cold packs. Try to keep your cooler in a shady place as well. To be sure that your food is safe, try to bring many items that do not require refrigeration or any type of special handling. Some good choices to take along when you go camping are:

- Peanut butter in plastic jars
- Concentrated juice boxes
- Dried noodles and soups
- Beef jerky and other dried meats
- Dried fruits and nuts
- Powdered milk and fruit drinks
- Packaged meals

Campers can get dirty quickly, but it is important to have clean hands when working with food wherever you are. If there is no running water near your campsite, bring your own tap water. If this is not convenient for you, use disinfectant wipes.

Also, be sure to bring your own tap water or bottled water to drink. Even if the water in the lakes, rivers, or streams near your campsite looks crystal clear, do not drink from these. Remember—you can't see the microbes that can make you very sick. As your water supply runs low, see if you can replenish it with water from a safe public water system nearby. If this isn't possible, camping stores sell water purification tablets and filters that you can use to make untreated water safe to drink.

www.usatoday.com

News
SECTION A

April 10, 2009

From the Pages of USA TODAY

Those 50 and older most vulnerable to food illnesses

Scientists have found, to their surprise, that people 50 and older are the most vulnerable to illness and death from food-borne illnesses.

The Centers for Disease Control and Prevention released the 2008 findings of its FoodNet reporting system Thursday. The CDC has tracked food-borne pathogens [disease carriers] since 1996.

Doctors thought children under 4 were more at risk because cases involving young kids are seen at much higher rates, CDC epidemiologist Kavita Trivedi says. But that could be because parents "get more nervous and so take their kids in," she says.

When the CDC did a more targeted analysis, it found that hospitalization and death rates are significantly higher for people 50 and older.

Of people infected with the *Listeria* bacteria, 86% of those 50 and older were hospitalized, compared with 52% of children under 4. For deadly strains of *E. coli*, 53% of those 50 and older were hospitalized vs. 31% of young kids. The comparison was 40% vs. 19% for *Salmonella*.

"As a physician, that tells me that I need to pay more attention to a patient over 50 who comes in with a food-borne illness," Trivedi says. What's behind the disparity between the age groups isn't known, she says.

The food industry needs to recognize that customers are aging and "less capable of handling hazards in the food supply," says Caroline Smith DeWaal, a food safety expert with the advocacy group Center for Science in the Public Interest.

That may mean changes to how food is handled and labeled and how outbreaks are dealt with, she says. "For example, we need to understand that older consumers may be more [reluctant to throw] food away."

Overall, the CDC found that there was no significant change from 2007 in the number of foodborne illnesses last year. The 10 FoodNet sites reported a total of 18,499 laboratory-confirmed cases of infection.

Compared with 1996–1998, there was a 25% decrease in the illnesses that FoodNet tracks, according to CDC's Morbidity and Mortality Report, which published the data.

—*Elizabeth Weise*

COOK AND EAT RESPONSIBLY

Whether you are at home or out and about, it is important to be aware of food safety. About sixteen thousand people become ill with foodborne diseases every day in the United States. About twenty-five of them die. Most often these are children, the elderly, or people who are already ill. In poorer, developing nations, where hygiene and sanitation are lax, the incidence of foodborne disease is still higher. In these areas, foodborne disease is often a major cause of serious illness, especially in very young children.

Foodborne disease can be costly on many levels, regardless of where it occurs. Besides the physical and emotional discomfort it causes, in severe cases, there can be high medical bills, as well as school or work time lost. According to the USDA, the annual cost of foodborne disease in terms of medical care, lost productivity, and premature deaths may run as high as $37 billion. Clearly, the prevention of foodborne disease should be everyone's concern.

GLOSSARY

agroterrorist: a terrorist who attacks agricultural products such as crops or livestock

antibiotic: a medication used to destroy or stop the growth of harmful microbes in the body

antitoxin: a medication used to fight the effects of a specific toxin that has been introduced into the body

bacteria: microscopic living things that can cause disease in some cases

botulism: a rare but extremely serious illness caused by a toxin produced by a bacteria called *Clostridium botulinum*

chlorine: a gas used to kill germs in water

coma: a state of deep prolonged unconsciousness resulting from an illness, injury, or poison

convulsion: an abnormal and involuntary muscular contraction of the body, as in a spasm or fit

cyst: a saclike structure filled with fluid or a somewhat solid material

degenerative disease: an illness that causes deterioration of function or structure

dehydration: suffering from a loss of water or body fluids

dementia: a condition characterized by deteriorating mental capacity

diagnosis: the act of identifying diseases and disorders from their symptoms

dialysis: a procedure to remove toxic substances in the blood as the result of poor kidney function

disinfect: to free from harmful bacteria

DNA (deoxyribonucleic acid): the molecule that contains genetic information and is passed from parent to offspring during reproduction. It is shaped like a spiraling ladder and is contained in the nucleus of most cells.

epidemiologist: a public health official who analyzes and treats disease outbreaks

hygienic: maintaining clean and healthy practices

immune system: the body system that provides protection against disease

incontinent: unable to control or hold back the discharge of urine or feces

incubation: the time period between being exposed to a germ and the appearance of symptoms of disease

infection: a harmful condition caused by disease-producing organisms

intravenous: injected directly into a vein

larvae: the early immature form of an insect or of some water animals that passes through several stages from which the adult eventually emerges

lesion: a sore or an infected patch of skin

mamey: a juicy tropical fruit with a hard rind

marinating: the process of placing a food in a spiced or flavored liquid to add flavor

meningitis: an inflammation of the membranes that surround the brain and spinal cord

microbes: disease-producing bacteria that are too small to be seen with the naked eye

paralysis: a partial or complete loss of sensation or movement in a part of the body

parasite: a plant or animal that lives off another living thing known as a host

respiratory: related to breathing

RNA (ribonucleic acid): a molecule similar to DNA that carries genetic information

stillbirth: dead at birth

toxin: a disease-causing poison produced by a living organism

vaccine: a substance injected or taken orally to create immunity to a specific disease

ventilator: a device to assist an individual who is having trouble breathing

virus: a tiny organism that reproduces and grows in living cells and causes disease

RESOURCES

Center for Food Safety
660 Pennsylvania Avenue SE, #302
Washington, DC 20003
202-547-9359
http://www.centerforfoodsafety.org

The Center for Food Safety is a nonprofit organization established for the purpose of challenging harmful food production technologies and promoting sustainable alternatives. The center uses multiple tools and strategies in pursuing its goals including legal action, public education, grassroots organizing, and media outreach.

Food Safety Information Center (FSIC)
National Agricultural Library/USDA
10301 Baltimore Avenue, Room 304
Beltsville, MD 20705-2351
301-504-5515
http://www.foodsafety.nal.usda.gov/

The Food Safety Information Center specializes in providing food safety information to educators, industry researchers, and the general public. It strives to develop strong collaborations among the USDA's National Agricultural Library's safety programs and ultimately deliver the best possible services to the food safety community. The center also includes the Food Safety Research Information Office that provides information and reference services to the research community.

National Restaurant Association Educational Foundation (NRAEF)
175 West Jackson Boulevard, Suite 1500
Chicago, IL 60604-2814
1-800-765-2122
http://www.nraef.org/

The National Restaurant Association Educational Foundation together with the National Restaurant Association provide education and networking opportunities to enable food providers to learn from one another. (The National Restaurant Association is the leading business association for the restaurant industry.) The NRAEF ServSafe Program provides the training resources to help keep food safety as an essential ingredient in every meal. The group also provides food safety and nutrition information on its website.

Safe Tables Our Priority (STOP)
914 Silver Spring Avenue, Suite 206
Silver Spring, MD 20910
301-585-STOP (7867)
http://www.safetables.org

STOP is a national, nonprofit public health organization dedicated to preventing illness and death from foodborne pathogens. It seeks to achieve its mission by advocating changes in public policy, educating and doing outreach, and providing assistance to victims of foodborne illness.

USDA/Center for Food Safety and Applied Nutrition (CFSAN)
5100 Branch Parkway
College Park, MD 20740
1-888-SAFEFOOD
http://www.cfsan.fda.gov/

The Center for Food Safety and Applied Nutrition is one of six product-oriented centers that carry out the mission of the Food and Drug Administration (FDA). CFSAN, in conjunction with the agency's field staff, is responsible for promoting and protecting the public's health by ensuring that the nation's food supply is safe, wholesome, and honestly labeled. The center is also involved in consumer education and community outreach regarding food safety practices.

SOURCE NOTES

27 Nancy Shute, "Stores Call Customers about Salmonella–Tainted Peanut Products," *U.S. News & World Report,* February 3, 2009, http://www.usnews .com/health/blogs/on-parenting/2009/02/03/stores-call-customers-about -salmonella-tainted-peanut-products.html (February 3, 2010).

89–91 Barack Obama, weekly address, Saturday, March 14, 2009, Washington, DC, available online at www.whitehouse.gov/blog/09/03/14/Food-Safety (February 16, 2010).

95 Christopher Lee, "Agency Seeks to Allay Nation's Fears about Food Supply," *Washington Post,* May 21, 2008, A2.

SELECTED BIBLIOGRAPHY

Ashenburg, Katherine. *The Dirt on Clean: An Unsanitized History*. New York: North Point Press, 2008.

Fox, Nicholas. *It Was Probably Something You Ate: A Practical Guide to Avoiding and Surviving Food-borne Illness*. New York: Penguin, 1999.

Green, Laura R. "Behavioral Science and Food Safety." *Journal of Environmental Health* Vol. 71, no. 2 (September 2008): 47.

Heersink, Mary. *E. coli O157: The True Story of a Mother's Battle with a Killer Microbe*. Far Hills, NJ: New Horizon Press, 1996.

Hester, R. E., and R. M. Harrison. *Food Safety and Food Quality*. London: Royal Society of Chemistry, 2001.

Journal of the American Dietetic Association, "Foodborne Illness Booklet." Vol. 100, no. 7 (July 2000): 855.

———. "Purdue Research Park-Based Company Detects and Traps Bacteria that Cause Foodborne Illness." Vol. 71, no. 5 (December 2008): 58.

McSwane, Davis, Richard Linton, and Nancy R. Rue. *Essentials of Food Safety and Sanitation*. 4th ed. Upper Saddle River, NJ: Prentice Hall, 2002.

Newbold, K. Bruce, Marie McKeary, Robert Hart, and Robert Hall. "Restaurant Inspection Frequency and Food Safety Compliance." *Journal of Environmental Health* Vol. 71, no. 4 (November 2008): 56.

Parry, Sharon, and Stephen Palmer. *E.coli: Environmental Health Issues of VTEC O157*. Oxford, UK: Taylor and Francis, 2002.

Rue, Nancy R. and Anna Graf Williams. *Quick Reference to Food Safety and Sanitation*. Upper Saddle River, NJ: Prentice Hall, 2002.

Sachs, Jessica Snyder. *Good Germs, Bad Germs: Health and Survival in a Bacterial World*. New York: Hill and Wang, 2008.

Satin, Morton. *Death in the Pot: The Impact of Food Poisoning on History*. Buffalo: Prometheus Books, 2007.

Smith, Virginia. *Clean: A History of Personal Hygiene and Purity*. Oxford: Oxford University Press, 2005.

Zimmer, Carl. *E. Coli and the New Science of Life*. New York: Pantheon Books, 2008.

FURTHER READING AND WEBSITES

Books
Brands, Danielle A. *Salmonella*. Philadelphia: Chelsea House, 2006.

Brynie, Faith Hickman. *101 Questions about Food and Digestion*. Minneapolis: Twenty-First-Century Books, 2002.

Emmeluth, Donald. *Botulism*. Philadelphia: Chelsea House, 2005.

Ferrerio, Carmen. *Mad Cow Disease*. Philadelphia: Chelsea House, 2004.

Fleisher, Paul. *Parasites*. Minneapolis: Twenty-First Century Books, 2006.

Friedlander, Mark P., Jr.. *Outbreak*. Minneapolis: Twenty-First Century Books, 2009.

Hempel, Sandra. *The Strange Case of the Broad Street Pump: John Snow and the Mystery of Cholera*. Berkeley: University of California Press, 2007.

Law, Bibiana. *Campylobacteriosis*. Philadelphia: Chelsea House, 2004.

Manning, Sharon. *Escherichia coli Infections, Second Edition*. Philadelphia: Chelsea House, 2010.

Peters, Stephanie True. *Cholera: Curse of the Nineteenth Century*. Tarrytown, NY: Benchmark Books, 2004.

Silverstein, Alvin, and Virginia Silverstein. *The Food Poisoning Update*. Berkley Heights, NJ: Enslow Publishers, 2007.

Websites
American Association of Poison Control Centers
www.aapcc.org/
This site contains information on how to find local poison control centers and what kinds of questions they answer, as well as other information about poisons and what to do if you are poisoned.

The Mayo Clinic – Botulism
http://www.mayoclinic.com/health/botulism/DS00657
The Mayo Clinic website has a section devoted to botulism that explains what it is, its symptoms, and how it is treated.

United States Department of Agriculture
www.usda.gov
The USDA website gives up-to-date information on food safety initiatives and what this government department is doing to monitor and ensure that food is safe and safely handled.

INDEX

ABOUT THE AUTHOR

Award-winning children's book author Elaine Landau worked as a newspaper reporter, a children's book editor, and a youth services librarian before becoming a full-time writer. She has written more than three hundred books for young readers. Among her recent titles are *Meth: America's Drug Epidemic*, The Best Dogs Ever series, and *Suicide Bombers: Foot Soldiers of the Terrorist Movement*, which was named a Notable Social Studies Trade Book for Young People 2007 by the National Council for the Social Studies (NCSS) and the Children's Book Council. Landau has a bachelor's degree in English and journalism from New York University and a master's degree in library and information science from Pratt Institute. She lives in Miami, Florida, with her husband and son.

PHOTO ACKNOWLEDGMENTS

The images in this book are used with the permission of: © S. Lowry/Univ Ulster/Stone/Getty Images, pp. 1, 3; © Romeo Ranoco/Reuters/CORBIS, p. 8; © David Zalubowski/USA TODAY, p. 10; © Dr. Dennis Kunkel/Visuals Unlimited, Inc., pp. 16, 42, 57, 63; © Bettmann/CORBIS, p. 18; © TopFoto/The Image Works, p. 23; © Elizabeth Weise/USA TODAY, p. 27; Centers for Disease Control and Prevention Public Health Image Library, pp. 35 (Janice Haney Carr), 38 (Janice Haney Carr), 45 (Charles D. Humphrey), 69 (DPDx - Melanie Moser), 71, 76 (Teresa Hammett); © Dr. Gary Gaugler/Visuals Unlimited, Inc., p. 41; © Comstock Images, p. 48; © Richard Kessel & Gene Shih/Visuals Unlimited, Inc., p. 50; AP Photo/The Oklahoman, Nate Billings, p. 54; © Dr. Fred Hossler/Visuals Unlimited, Inc., p. 60; © Dave Schlabowske/Time & Life Pictures/Getty Images, p. 68; © PHANIE/Photo Researchers, Inc., p. 81; © Keystone/Hulton Archive/Getty Images, p. 82; The Granger Collection, New York, p. 85; Agricultural Research Service, USDA/Keith Weller, p. 89; AP Photo/Damian Dovarganes, File, p. 91; © David R. Frazier Photolibrary, Inc./Alamy, p. 97; © Katye Martens/USA TODAY, p. 102; © Martin Jenkinson/Alamy, p. 105; AP Photo/Nati Harnik, p. 113.

Cover: © S. Lowry/Univ Ulster/Stone/Getty Images (main); © iStockphoto.com/Andrey Prokhorov (background).